GENE KRUPA
The Pictorial Life of a Jazz Legend

DR. BRUCE H. KLAUBER

ON THE COMPANION CD

Track	Title	Time
1	Wire Brush Stomp (drum solo) (1938) .... Gene Krupa, drums	2:30
2	Stompin' at the Savoy (1945) .... Gene Krupa, drums; Charlie Ventura, tenor saxophone; Teddy Napoleon, piano	4:45
3	Idaho (1953) .... Gene Krupa, drums; Charlie Ventura, tenor saxophone; Teddy Napoleon, piano	4:03
4	Dark Eyes (1953) .... Gene Krupa, drums; Charlie Ventura, tenor saxophone; Teddy Napoleon, piano	3:50
5	Steve Allen Segment (1955) .... Interview with Gene Krupa Indiana Krupa's Blues Gene Krupa, drums; Steve Allen, piano; with the Steve Allen Show house orchestra	6:52
6	Sing Sing Sing (1960) .... Gene Krupa, drums; Eddie Wasserman, reeds; Ronnie Ball, piano; Jimmy Gannon, bass	6:04
7	Leave Us Leap (1971) .... Gene Krupa, drums; with the Guido Basso Orchestra	3:33
8	Perdido (1971) .... Gene Krupa, drums; with Al Winters and the Six-Star International Jazz Band	10:35

For more information about the tracks on the CD, please see page 175.

Alfred Publishing Co., Inc.
Los Angeles

GENE KRUPA
THE PICTORIAL LIFE
OF A JAZZ LEGEND

Dr. Bruce H. Klauber

Library of Congress Cataloging-in-Publication Data

Klauber, Bruce H., 1952-
  Gene Krupa : the pictorial life of a jazz legend / Bruce H. Klauber.
    p. cm.
  ISBN 0-7390-3858-3 (book and cd)
1. Krupa, Gene, 1909-1973--Pictorial works. I. Title.

  ML419.K78K59 2005
  786.9'165'092--dc22

                                        2005022946

Interior Design and Layout **Dancing Planet® MediaWorks™**

ISBN 0-7390-3858-3 (Book & CD)

CONTENTS

4

FOREWORD

by Bobby Scott

In 1954, I got a call from Gene Krupa asking if I might enjoy playing piano in a new quartet he was forming, after his old trio of Charlie Ventura and Teddy Napoleon had disbanded for traveling reasons. I jumped at the chance and it began on a good note when I went to half-audition, half-learn his "book" of tunes he'd been using with the trio. Eddie Shu, the saxophonist/trumpeter, had bitched to Gene that he wouldn't play in a bass-less group and the Ol' Man (as all players traditionally refer to the leader) acquiesced to a quartet instead of a trio.

When I strolled into the Basin Street West nightclub that afternoon, I was delighted to see my good friend (and the guy I used in my own trio) Gordon "Whitey" Mitchell standing on the bandstand with Krupa and Shu. It boded well because Whitey was a first-class player and a first-class human being, too. Although he labored under being the younger brother of Red Mitchell, a highly regarded and gifted bassist, Whitey had his own way of playing and his own vision of how things ought to go down.

The drummer himself made an unusual apology to me on that first occasion we played together. After we'd finished rehearsing of a sort (everything was loose in that group!), he spoke to me of money, which wasn't great but would do, and then he said something that lifted him ten stories in my estimation. "I know you'd rather play with a Max Roach or an Art Blakey, and my playing is a bit old hat," Gene said to me. "But I'm ready to adjust to you young chaps and make the playing something we can all enjoy doing." I was, to say the least, taken aback. It was the first time I'd ever heard words of an apologetic nature from someone who need hardly say them. And to a young fool like me? But that was only my first indication of how amenable the Ol' Man was about things in general. I must have run into him at a most propitious time in his working life.

On not a few occasions he expressed a longing for the joys he'd experienced with his big bands of the past. But then his near-immediate afterthought was, "But it was taking 15 kids to camp, Chappie. I don't think I could handle the human hassling that one has to, running a pack of young players." Dealing with Eddie, Whitey, and me was about as much as Gene wanted on his plate.

Gene was one of the loveliest people I met among the players. A very small man—his drumming belied his size—but not fragile. Short of stature, and at a later time in his life rather spindly-legged. He carried himself well, and if I'm to believe him, he had matured much later than he'd wanted to. He was the first truly successful player I'd met who warned me, in dire terms, to be careful of success. It was "a killer," he sadly noted to me one day while traveling. "The hardest thing to do, Chappie, is to mellow with the success that comes to you," he told me. "But few people ever do." I know he was speaking about himself, to begin with, but he cited others for me, and the aberrations that accompanied their ascent up the ladder of success. The last thing you could say about the Ol' Man was that he graced you with meaningless platitudes. No, he didn't waste himself preaching, and, God knows, as wild and woolly as I was at that time, I could have used some of it. But he made his points simply and succinctly. He could never be accused of saying too much.

I learned a valuable lesson watching him turn on his social side and smile in response to the many fans who longed to be in his company, if even for a few seconds. It was never disingenuous either. It was as if he pushed a lever somewhere that threw overboard all of his personal cares for the moment, and he genuinely engaged the party before him. Most of his diehard fans found a source of encouragement in his very presence as they, no doubt, reflected upon his imprisonment and his re-emergence as a performer of the first order. Unlike many other musicians, Gene had an entertainment value because of his manner of playing, which drew in an audience rather than puzzled them.

That he was proud of his past accomplishments is taken for granted. Wasn't he the fire that drove the Goodman orchestra up the hill to Olympus? Benny [Goodman] wouldn't admit it to be the truth, but I know better. For me, as a young listener, "Sing Sing Sing" meant Krupa's drumming.

I'll miss you, Ol' Man.

Bobby Scott was a jazz pianist, vocalist, arranger, and composer—his most well-known compositions are "A Taste of Honey" and "He Ain't Heavy, He's My Brother"—who was a member of the Gene Krupa Quartet in 1954 and 1955. Scott was just 17 when he joined Gene, whom he fondly called "Ol' Man." He became quite attached to Krupa, and in his later years Scott would write warmly about the experience for a number of publications. At the time of his death in 1990, Bobby Scott was putting the finishing touches on his autobiography. He gave me a copy of the work, which he officially titled With Never a Crack in My Heart: A Memoir. *I know Bob would have been happy to see a part of it in book form as the foreword to this work. —Bruce Klauber*

SPECIAL THANKS

A project of this scope does not happen by itself. Many fine people are owed a debt of gratitude. I extend this gratitude and a very special thanks to Ray Brych and Dave Olsen for their faith in me and my ideas; Paul Testa and Louis Bernstein, dear friends and great drummers who have freely shared their unbelievable Gene Krupa and Buddy Rich collections with me through the years; Bob Bierman, a Krupa collector and appreciator from day one; Krupa friend Gilbert Yule, responsible for many of Gene's latter-day bookings with regional jazz bands; KYDD bass inventor and Drexel University instructor Bruce Kaminsky for his friendship and good humor; University of the Arts' Marc Dicciani and Don Glanden for their dedication to jazz scholarship and good writing; and Frances Klauber and Joel Klauber for giving me the gift of music.

I doff my cap to my supporters in Europe for their ideas, input, and good fellowship, including Patrice Bertin of France; Maxwell Gunn, Peter Brightman, and Alex Richmond of England; and Akira Suzuki of Japan.

Mention must be made of "the other Bruce," my friend and great writer Bruce Growther, who has done so much in the way of ensuring that Gene receives the credit he deserves.

My "French connection," Patrice Bertin, let me know about a new Krupa "package" from *Editions Nocturne* of France as a part of their BD Jazz Series. This two-CD set comes with a 26-page book of color drawings by Olivier Desvaux that literally tell the Gene Krupa story. My thanks to Patrice for his help in gaining permission from the Nocturne company and Bruno Theol to use a few frames from this project. Authors, historians and drummers Rob Cook and Jon Cohan have done much to enrich jazz and drumming scholarship through their fine books. Their information was invaluable to me.

One of the truly satisfying things about writing and producing drum DVDs has been discovering that the greatest drummers playing today have a great deal of respect for and knowledge of the jazz and drumming tradition. My contemporary colleagues, who have taken the time to contribute their thoughts and comments on Gene, all deserve a long drum roll. They are: Phil Collins, Neil Peart, David Garibaldi, John Blackwell, Peter Criss, Carmine Appice, Carl Palmer, Alphonse Mouzon, Kenny Aronoff, Ed Shaughnessy, Peter Erskine, Tommy Aldridge, Alex Acuña, and "Professor" Steve Smith. These players, each in their own individual way, exemplify talent, skill, and versatility and, like Gene, have an unparalleled love for the instrument. They are all giants and I am proud to know them and to have worked with them.

Finally, I extend all the love and thanks possible in this universe—and beyond—to Joy Adams, who has made everything good in my life possible.

ABOUT THE PHOTOGRAPHS

As the first "matinee idol" ever produced by jazz, Gene Krupa had to be among the most photographed artists in improvisational music history. Everyone through the years, it seemed, wanted to take his picture, which explains the many candid shots of "that ace drummer man" in action in this collection.

The advertising, publicity and exploitation departments of record companies, motion picture studios, theaters, radio networks and ballrooms—to say nothing of Krupa's own marketing people—were vast "machines" in the 1930s, the 1940s and into the 1950s. They sent out hundreds of still photos of Gene and many other eminently photographable bandleaders each year, in hopes that they would be published in the newspapers, magazines, music trades like *Downbeat* and *Metronome*, and *Orchestra World*, and fanzines like *Bandleaders*. Many of the pictures in this work come from those sources. In those days, photographers simply weren't credited for picture works—thank goodness they are today. The companies just wanted them *published*. Consider it done.

Gene Krupa was likely the most loyal and undemanding endorser that the Avedis Zildjian Cymbal Company and the Slingerland Drum Company ever had. He used their products exclusively for almost 40 years, and hardly ever requested anything.

Mel Tormé was always fond of telling the story about Slingerland's people almost having to *force* Gene to accept new drums and cases. A good amount of the graphics within come from Zildjian, Slingerland and some of the other few products Gene chose to endorse.

Here's hoping that Slingerland's "comeback" is successful. As for Zildjian, their cymbals remain "the only serious choice."

Over the years and with my various Gene Krupa projects, I've been lucky enough to have been given permission and rights to use a number of publicity stills from the Duncan Schiedt and Frank Driggs' collections; the late Robert Asen, one-time publisher of *Metronome* magazine; the late *Downbeat* magazine president Jack Maher; *Modern Drummer* magazine's late founder and publisher Ronald Spagnardi; and the late Mel Tormé. I miss them and I thank them.

Every reasonable step has been taken to find out whether or not present copyright holders of this material exist. Dozens of collectors, it seems, have the same photo or photos in their collections. If someone was unintentionally left out, you have my advance apologies and my promise that you will be acknowledged properly in any subsequent work similar to this one.

INTRODUCTION

When Mel Tormé, rest his soul, was approached 13 years ago about contributing the introduction to my book, *World of Gene Krupa: That Legendary Drummin' Man*, he offered only one piece of advice to the author. "Kid," he said, "whatever you do, use lots of photos, especially that killer picture of Gene sweating through his jacket at the Savoy Ballroom. Always remember that Gene was *visual*."

Mel was right. While Gene Krupa's artistry was *heard* on his thousands of classic recordings, the consensus of opinion is that he had to be *seen* to be really appreciated. Some have described Gene's visual appeal—the flying hair, the ferocious gum chewing, the array of facial expressions, and the lighting gimmicks, etc.—as showmanship. Gene called it "projecting to an audience," and he was obviously quite successful in projecting the message of good jazz to the masses. Many of the legions of Krupa fans will be happy to say that they didn't like jazz before or since Gene. But his way of projecting wasn't affected or put-on, either. John Bunch, his pianist through much of the 1960s, once told me that Gene used the same facial expressions in rehearsal as he did on the job. What audiences saw and felt was Gene's simple enthusiasm for jazz. He loved it, and it showed.

Since the publication of *World of Gene Krupa* in 1990, the marketplace has been flooded with Krupa CDs, shirts, posters, sticks, drum sets, reissues of his drum instruction books, tribute recordings, tribute concerts, web sites, more than one "Gene Krupa Orchestra," and the two DVDs on Gene, *Gene Krupa: Jazz Legend* and *Gene Krupa: Swing, Swing, Swing*. Krupa memorabilia is a cottage industry on eBay. His place as a certifiable jazz innovator has been solidified. And the theme song of the recent swing craze? None other than Gene's feature with Benny Goodman, "Sing, Sing, Sing". Every other television commercial these days seems to be using some version of it.

Consider *Gene Krupa: The Pictorial Life of a Jazz Legend* to be another tribute, this one photographic. Drummers of a certain age particularly miss the era of the long-playing record album, mainly because of the great photos on the front and back of the record jacket. Countless famous and not-so-famous percussionists remember a time when they could *hold* the album cover, look at that picture of Gene or Buddy for hours and hours, then go in the other room and set up their drums just like they were set up in the picture. Compact discs? A CD may hold more music, but the package itself just doesn't give that same feeling.

Among the most frequent requests we've received over the years is for photos or posters of Gene. Perhaps people just want to *hold* the pictures again, or wonder what it was like to have been there, or just to see how Gene Krupa set up his drums. These photographs capture that "ace drummer man" through five decades, from the 1930s to the 1970s, in various poses and moods. The aim of the accompanying commentary is to place the photo in musical and historical perspective. Each image tells a tale of what was going on in Gene's life, in his music, in jazz, and in the development of the drumset.

Each photo has something in common, and that is Gene's love for the instrument and for jazz. And if you listen very closely while holding one of these pictures, you might just hear the sound of drums.

TODAY'S DRUMMERS ON GENE KRUPA

"My memories of Gene Krupa go all the way back to before I started playing the drums at nine years old in 1963. My folks had some Benny Goodman sides and I remember my mom playing "Sing, Sing, Sing" and getting into the drum solo. When I started studying with Billy Flanagan, a great 'local' teacher in the Boston area, he talked about Gene, Buddy and Louie, the 'Big Three.' He made sure I listened to all of them and I loved that style of playing—it totally shaped my early years. Now I know that Gene was first and he influenced Buddy, and they both influenced Louie, but in those days I just knew they all sounded amazing!

I had heard there was movie about Gene Krupa, and before the days of video and DVD it was hard to see a particular movie. You had to wait for it to be on TV. I remember searching the *TV Guide* for *The Gene Krupa Story*—one day I found it! Yes, the movie was going to broadcast, but of course it was on late at night, way after my bedtime. I waited in my bed until everyone in the house was asleep and I snuck downstairs in the middle of the night to see *The Gene Krupa Story*. I just *loved* every minute of that movie. I have since found out that there isn't much fact in the movie, it was mainly Hollywood fiction, but still—how great that there was a Hollywood movie made about a *drummer*!

Obviously he probably had the best 'showmanship' of any drummer that ever lived, but he was a superb musician as well. As a big band drummer, Gene had a subtle approach, mainly supporting the band with driving, swinging time and not many fills. When the time came for a fill or solo, it jumped out in an exciting and musically appropriate way. When playing with a small group, Gene had a very complimentary and melodic approach to the music, something that I didn't notice in his playing until I was old enough to appreciate it.

Sadly, I never did get to see him play live. My mom and dad took a trip to New York City one weekend and they came back raving about seeing Gene at the Metropole. I was so jealous because they went on and on about what a small and intimate club it was, how they got to sit very close to the stage, how the music was great, that they talked to Gene after the show and he was such a gentleman, blah, blah, blah! I wished I had gone too! Thankfully there are some fantastic film and TV clips of Gene that we can now see and get a close-up view of one of the greatest drummers that who ever lived."

—*Steve Smith (Journey, Vital Information, Buddy's Buddies)*

"Besides tiny Chick Webb and 'Big' Sid Catlett, no one ever noticed the drummer in the band until Gene Krupa came along. He was really the first to make people sit up and listen to 'the drum solo'. His charisma and ability encouraged other players to lead from the back of the stage. Probably, without him, people might not be taking drummers so seriously today. Though he wasn't possibly as technically breathtaking as Buddy Rich, even Buddy would admit that Krupa was the first, the originator of all that followed. We drummers owe him a lot."

—*Phil Collins (Genesis, solo artist, singer, composer)*

"Gene Krupa was more than just a famous drummer/bandleader. He was an innovator; a pioneer. He was the first to bring drums to the front of the stage. And. . . he could actually play. In this day and age those attributes seem mutually exclusive. It's rare enough to hear a drummer with exceptional facility, but to be just as impressed with what you *see* makes it even more compelling. This epitomizes what Krupa was. He attacked your ears and your eyes relentlessly. Consequently, it was impossible for him to inhabit anywhere but front and center. I am familiar with his recordings and they are impressive enough. But what Gene Krupa *really* was, could only be conveyed on film. He grabbed you by the scruff of the neck and snatched you into what he was doing. There was no way to ignore Gene Krupa, and it's that way still. I thank him for all he's done for drums and drumming. God bless ya GK!"

—*Tommy Aldridge (Gary Moore, Whitesnake, Ozzy Osbourne)*

"Gene Krupa is my hero. He was one of the first jazz drummers I ever heard when I was starting to learn to play jazz. I was 15 (now 30…ha ha!), and I saw this television special on big bands. One of the big bands was Gene Krupa. Man, I tell you, he was on fire. His stick and arm movements and 'arm in the air freezes' just caught my attention. One thing that I learned from Gene is that you don't have to do a lot of 'chops' to capture an audience. As a matter of fact, when you do less, they'll go wild. That's what Gene did whenever he did a solo and in some of his most famous drum battles with Buddy Rich and many other greats. *But he made up with what he didn't do with showmanship*, and that, my friends, is the icing on the cake. Gene was also the first superstar drummer. He took the drums from behind the scenes and brought it to the front of the stage. Thank you Gene and God bless you."

—*John Blackwell (Patti LaBelle, Robert Newton and Lotusfete, Prince)*

"When I was six years old, I finally had the opportunity to meet drumming legend Gene Krupa. He was appearing at the Steel Pier Ballroom in Atlantic City, and my oldest sister, Lois (who was 15 at the time), took me to see him play. When she saw where his dressing room was located, she took me in tow and knocked on his door. He was alone in the room and answered, kindly inviting us in. She did a short song and dance routine about how I was this terrific young drummer and Gene finally said, as he handed me a pair of drumsticks and pointed to a chair, 'Show me what you can do, kid.' I had never played on a wooden chair before, but I gulped, grabbed the sticks and fumbled something on the seat of the chair's surface with Mr. Krupa's drumsticks. When I looked up at him, Gene Krupa smiled, nodded his head and said, 'Yeah, kid. . . yeah!' Gene played a knockout set at that afternoon matinee, and gave this kid drummer a memorable moment he would never forget."

—*Peter Erskine (Stan Kenton, Maynard Ferguson, Weather Report, Steps Ahead, author, clinician) Excerpted with permission from Peter Eskine's book* Drum Essentials Volume 3,"*Alfred Publishing.*

"Along with his unique brilliance at drumming, Gene Krupa had the kindest, most generous spirit toward younger drummers. He made me, and many others, feel so good with encouragement and compliments, especially during those early insecure years. I loved him for that."

—*Ed Shaughnessy (Big Band legend, author, clinician, The Tonight Show Orchestra)*

"When a drummer comes up to me and tells me he plays drums because of me, I say 'Holy shit…thank you!' I play drums because of Gene Krupa. The first time I heard "Sing, Sing, Sing", a record my dad put on when I was a boy, I knew right then and there that I wanted to be the guy on that record. After some years, I got to see and hear the great man play. Along with my dearest friend, NY Dolls' drummer Jerry Nolan, who has passed on, I saw him at a place called the Metropole Café on 57th Street in New York City. He was everything I imagined and more. After seeing and hearing him play, I wanted to be him! If not for GK, I would not be who I am today. I can't wait to jam with him in heaven."

—*Peter Criss (Gene Krupa student, Kiss)*

"Gene Krupa not only inspired me because of his technique and musicality, but also for his ability to perform with so much passion and excitement. His tech-nique and creative ideas behind the drum set never got in the way of the music he was playing. He brought the drum set to the front of the band, and made people aware of how creative the drummer in a band can be."

—*Kenny Aronoff (John Cougar Mellencamp, Elton John, Rod Stewart, Melissa Etheridge, et. al., author, clinician)*

"Gene Krupa was an incredible drummer. He was also great for drumming because of his impeccable ability to ostentatiously play the drums, and because of his charming good looks, which attracted a lot of beautiful females. (I know that first-hand from my drumming experiences about attracting beautiful ladies.) Gene influenced me so much that I played a drum intro solo in the Tom Hanks' film *That Thing You Do* that was similar to the style of Gene Krupa. Gene was one of the greatest drummers in the world."

—*Alphonse Mouzon (McCoy Tyner, Weather Report, composer, actor)*

"At the tender age of 11 years, I went to see *Drum Crazy*. That was the name of the film at the time in the U.K. To the rest of the world it was *The Gene Krupa Story* and I was hooked! When I walked out of the movie theater with my father I knew I had been directed down a path that I would follow for the rest of my life, and that was to be a drummer. Forty three years later, I am still walking down that path thanks to Gene Krupa."

—*Carl Kendall-Palmer (Emerson Lake and Palmer, PM, Asia, Palmer)*

"When I was a kid, my parents took me to see *The Gene Krupa Story*, which starred Sal Mineo. This was in 1959 and I

was in the 8th grade. The drumming in the movie, actually done by Gene Krupa himself, was awesome, and got me really excited about playing. My first year in college, a drummer friend of mine (Rich Quintanal, who played in the Don Ellis band) and I took a photo with our drum sets facing each other, just like on the cover of the Gene Krupa and Buddy Rich *Drum Battle* record. Gene helped to bring the drums to the front of the band, and gave importance to the role of the drummer in modern music."
—*David Garabaldi (Tower of Power, Natalie Cole, The Yellowjackets, author, clinician)*

"Gene Krupa was my *main* influence growing up. I had the Krupa and Rich *Drum Battle* album. I learned every solo that they both did on that record (Rich's solos were harder to learn). I used to see Gene on television in black and white. I saw *The Gene Krupa Story* movie in theaters three times. I had the soundtrack to the movie. I knew every note on that soundtrack. Yes, Gene was it. I even stole some ideas from the movie, where he played a tom rhythm and the band answered him until there were three tom patterns happening. Then Gene did a solo over the tom jungle rhythms. It was amazing. I did this on an album called *Cactus* in my solo on the song "Feel So Good". I had the guitar and bass playing the tom patterns and I did a solo to it. I also did this concept on my solo album in 1982, and I used to do this at clinics, bringing drummers up to play these tom patterns and I would solo over them. I used to look at the movie and try and base my career off of it. I wanted to be the 'Gene Krupa of Rock.' I actually saw Gene play once, at the Metropole Café in New York. That was at the end of his career. I got the whole idea of twirling and showmanship from Gene. *He was the original showman of the drums.* He brought the drums out front so people would appreciate them. Drumming would be totally different if he weren't around. *I love him! He was the best.*"
—*Carmine Appice (Vanilla Fudge, Pink Floyd, Jeff Beck, Ozzy Osbourne, author, clinician)*

"When I was growing up in Peru a long time ago I used to listen to Gene Krupa a lot. When Sal Mineo played Gene in The Gene Krupa Story, there I was at the movies, always a follower of Gene Krupa. I also had the privilege of witnessing his playing one evening in New York City, on Broadway at the Metropole Café, in April, 1964. I still remember it very clearly what happened to me that evening when I went to see Gene. They didn't allow me to sit inside the bar because I was underage. I was still in my teens. I had just arrived from Peru that day and went to walk around the city. I thought that in New York I could do the same things I did when I lived in Lima. In Lima, you can get inside of any bar or place that serves liquor if there is live music playing. Oh well. So, I just stayed around outside of the Metropole and I climbed over the cars and car bumpers, I stood up, and I still got the chance to see Gene Krupa, always smiling, playing his great rhythms with lots of joy."
—*Alex Neciosup Acuña (Weather Report, Wayne Shorter, Whitney Houston, Tito Puente, producer, educator and clinician)*

THE EARLY YEARS
1909-1934

Eugene Bertram Krupa was born January 15, 1909, in Chicago. He was the ninth and final child, with two girls and six boys coming ahead of him. "We originated the generation gap," Gene once said. "My oldest sister was 23 years older than me."

When Gene was 11, he worked with his brother Pete as a "chore boy" at the Brown Music Company on Chicago's South Side. "I wanted into music," Gene recalled years later, "and drums just happened to be the cheapest instrument in the wholesale catalog. After I made the purchase, I played at every opportunity. The sticks almost never left my hand."

His mother had hoped he would be a priest, and sent him to St. Joseph's College. Though Gene would later credit the school's Father, Ildefonse Rapp, for teaching him music appreciation, the drive for music was too strong and he left St. Joseph's to finish high school in Chicago.

By 1926, he was working in and around Chicago with a number of commercial outfits like the Seattle Harmony Kings and the Hoosier Bell Hops. His jazz career began in earnest on December 9, 1927. Along with (Red) McKenzie and (Eddie) Condon's Chicagoans, Gene cut four tracks which were said to be the first known records to include the use of the bass drum. The songs were "China Boy", "Sugar", "Nobody's Sweetheart" and "Liza". A year later, Gene and some of his Chicago cohorts made the move to New York, with a promise of work coming from vaudeville singer and "hot music" fan Bea Palmer. The job didn't work out.

Some record dates and single engagements began to materialize, with included now-historic sessions with Red Nichols, Wingy Manone, Bud Freeman, Fats Waller and many more. By the end of 1928, he was a member of the Red Nichols Orchestra.

The Nichols group served as the pit orchestra for the Broadway shows *Strike Up the Band* and *Girl Crazy*. At that time, Gene couldn't read a note of music and depended on fellow orchestra member Glenn Miller to signal him when to start and stop. "Right then and there," Gene said, "I resolved to learn the drums technically from the bottom up. I got myself the best teacher, Sanford 'Gus' Moeller, in New York and started in." Another major part of his percussion education was his exposure to giants like Ellington's Sonny Greer and especially Chick Webb.

Though very much involved with jazz, Gene still had to make a living, and played with a number of sweet bands like Irving Aaronson's Commanders, Mal Hallet, and a group fronted by singer Russ Columbo. The Columbo group was actually put together by someone named Benny Goodman.

Two years later, Goodman's own jazz-oriented band was shaping up.

They had a 26-week contract for the NBC radio program, *Let's Dance*, which began airing in December of 1934. The drummer, Stan King, just wasn't swinging. Goodman friend and talent scout John Hammond had the perfect player in mind. Krupa was playing with the rather commercial Buddy Rogers band (Rogers, star of early motion pictures, was supposedly able to play all the instruments in the band "equally lousy," Krupa recalled), at Chicago's College Inn, and Hammond paid him a visit and Gene Krupa joined the Benny Goodman band shortly after. The exact date Krupa joned up? Reports through the years have varied, but Goodman expert D. Russell Connor has pinpointed it as December 22, 1934.

Gene (left) about age five or six in Chicago with brother Julius.

That's brother Jules at the wheel of the cycle that belonged to brother Pete. Gene, age seven, is in the sidecar.

• AT 9—WITH BROTHER JULIUS (RIGHT) AND A FRIEND IN CHICAG

*Gene (center) in 1919 with brother Julius (right) and a
friend in Chicago.*

Gene (right) with brother Pete (left) and Julius.

Dig those crazy knickers! A 13-year-old Gene (third from the left) with brother Pete (to Gene's left) and friends.

Outside of Atlantic City's Steel Pier with Mal Hallett's Orchestra, 1933. Gene is eighth from the left. The Steel Pier marquee remained pretty much the same until it closed in the late 1970s.

THE BENNY GOODMAN ERA 1934-1938

Big-band jazz had been around long before Benny Goodman was crowned its "King." Duke Ellington and Fletcher Henderson had expanded jazz-oriented ensembles in 1924; Benny Moten led one with Count Basie as its pianist beginning in 1929; and Don Redman began as a leader around 1931. There were many more of what could be called "big bands" on local, regional and territorial levels. Still, the *real* Benny Goodman story—not the movie—has become the stuff of folklore and legend. The Goodman band *was* the swing era to the public at large, and represented a period of time when jazz— maybe for the first and last time in American musical history—was the popular music of the day. No, Goodman didn't create big band jazz, but like Gene, he synthesized all that he had heard before, applied his superior technical skills as a clarinetist, rehearsed that band until it was tight as a Radio King snare drum, and hired soloists who had no technical equals on their instruments. They *swung*. Gene's enthusiasm, his showmanship and his ability to *project* really helped sell the band.

"Benny had a tough time getting started," Gene once explained when asked about Goodman's beginnings. "I remember when we played Elitch's Gardens in

Denver, that we never had more than five people on the dance floor. One night, Benny laid out a lot of rhumbas. I said, 'Look, Benny, I'm making $85 a week with you, and if you're going commercial, I might as well go back to Buddy Rogers and make $125 a week. Let's stick to your original idea even if we go under.' Benny did and week later at the Palomar in Los Angeles, we clicked for good."

There were many triumphs, including a long stand at the Congress Hotel in Chicago, the famed, "dancing-the-aisles" pandemonium at the Paramount Theater in New York city of March, 1937; the superb recordings of what was the first racially mixed musical group to appear before a wide American public (The Goodman Trio with pianist Teddy Wilson, and later a quartet with vibraphonist Lionel Hampton); a couple of motion picture appearances, and of course, the Carnegie Hall Concert of January 16, 1938.

Gene had become a certifiable star, and the first matinee idol ever produced by jazz. In reality, he was still a sideman, but a sideman who was rapidly commanding more attention than the leader. Agents were after Krupa to form his own outfit, audiences were screaming for more drum solos, and Gene's playing had become more geared to the audience than to the band.

The big Goodman-Krupa "blowup" occurred during an engagement at Philadelphia's Earle Theater, which took place from February 26 to March 3 of 1938. Those who were there claimed the men were feuding openly on stage. Krupa quit on March 3 and it was an event that shocked the music world. On April 16, Gene premiered as the leader of his own band at The Steel Pier in Atlantic City. Over 4,000 fans were in the audience to cheer him on.

Benny and Gene in happier days, around 1936.

Filming of the motion picture The Big Broadcast of 1937 *in July of 1936.*

Two views of the Krupa photo that Mel Tormé described as "a killer." These were taken at a Chick Webb–Benny Goodman "battle of the bands," held on May 11, 1937 at the Savoy Ballroom. Chick's band carved Goodman's, and Chick's drumming overshadowed Gene's. "I was never cut by a better man," Gene said afterwards. Note that the tom-toms, though tunable top and bottom (something Gene insisted on and helped the Slingerland Drum Company create and devise), were still not using actual lugs. And the splash cymbal looks like the Chinese variety and not a Zildjian.

This view has Goodman star trumpeter Harry James to Gene's right. The bassist is Benny's brother, Harry.

Gene going over the charts during the filming of the 1937 motion picture Hollywood Hotel. *Benny, as usual, is preoccupied changing a reed.*

The full Goodman band as they appeared in Hollywood Hotel.

The Benny Goodman Trio, with Teddy Wilson on piano, before the Hollywood Hotel *cameras. By this time, while the toms had separate tension and real lugs, the bass drum didn't. The hoop mounted cymbal holder isn't holding so well, either.*

The Benny Goodman Quartet with Lionel Hampton on vibraphone, in Hollywood Hotel. *Many southern theater owners objected to the racially mixed group that appeared on screen, and made sure this sequence was cut before it was shown in their local movie house. Gene was not yet using the matching, white marine pearl drum throne, but whatever he's sitting on, his the initials "G.K." are on the side. Look at the radical angle of the snare drum, which appears to be a 6.5-inch model.*

Gene and Benny in the small group, from Hollywood Hotel. *This sequence may have been cut from the film. Gene often used a separate set for the trio and quartet, with a second rack tom added in place of a floor tom-tom. Who said the double, rack-mounted toms were a new idea? These, of course, were hoop-mounted, as was everything else at that time.*

The Benny Goodman Quartet, or "Quartette" as it says on the bass drum, at the Hollywood Hotel *filming.*

DRUMMER GENE KRUPA GOES TO TOWN TO THE TUNE OF WILTING HAIR, BEDRAGGLED TIE AND A FRENZY WHICH LEAVES HIM BATHED IN PERSPIRATION

Photo layout of Gene in various moods, late 1937, still using the old tension system on the bass drum. Gene received a lot of this type of attention—separate from the rest of the Goodman band—and it couldn't have made Benny happy.

Closeup from the same photo session from previous page.

Two years after the split, in 1940, Benny Goodman (right) poses with two of his former sidemen he helped make stars: Harry James and Gene Krupa.

THE FIRST BAND 1938-1943

T he quote has been used time and again, but no one has described the first public appearance of Gene's new band better than George T. Simon, who wrote about it in the May, 1938, issue of *Metronome* magazine. "In the neighborhood of four thousand, neighborhood and visiting cats scratched and clawed for points of vantage in the Marine Ballroom of Atlantic City's Steel Pier on Saturday, April 16, and then, once perched on their pet posts, proceeded to welcome with most exuberant howls and huzzahs the first public appearance of drummer-man Gene Krupa and his newly-formed jazz band. [There is] little doubt that Gene is now firmly entrenched at the helm of a new swing outfit that's bound to be recognized as one of the most potent bits of catnip ever to be fed to the purring public that generally passes as America's swing contingent."

Truth be told, while the first band was a well-rehearsed ensemble with some good soloists, its leader later admitted that too many of their songs featured drum solos, and that the band was often too loud. With singers like scat innovator Leo Watson, Irene Daye (the vocalist on the original version of Krupa hit "Drum Boogie"), some changes in personnel and a more varied book, the band began to have an identity of its own. With the arrival of trumpeter Roy Eldridge and singer Anita O' Day in 1941, the Krupa band became a genuine *star* attraction, with hit records (*Let Me Off Uptown, Rockin' Chair and Thanks For the Boogie Ride* among them), film appearances like *Ball of Fire* with Barbara Stanwyck in 1941, regular radio air shots and dates in the best locations. Krupa's first orchestra had a number of great players who passed through it, including saxophonists Charlie Ventura (who would have an association with Gene for more than 30 years), Sam

Donahue and Vido Musso; pianist and early bopper Dodo Marmorosa; trumpeters Corky Cornelius and Shorty Sherock; trombonist Tommy Pederson; and singer Johnny Desmond. Gene's arrangers during those years included Chappie Willett, Benny Carter, Elton Hill and Jimmy Mundy.

All of this success came to a crashing halt on January 18, 1943, and Gene Krupa's life would never be the same.

One of Gene's first formal publicity photos after he left the Goodman band. This has got to be one of the largest bass drums ever to exist in a drum set. Check out those stand-mounted spotlights to his left and right. Gene used some version of them until the end of his career. During his big drum solo, the lights in the room were turned out, Gene turned the spots on himself with a foot switch. The result was the famed "shadow effect." This could have been the first "light show" associated with music!

GK in a more serious vein with all separate tension lugs, but still showing light-duty, hoop-mounted hardware. The finger cymbal and "side" mounted cymbal were played with brushes or for special effects. Cymbals were so thin in those days that they often bent quite easily. Note the bent splash.

A more formal view, with Gene half-standing behind the set. A feature of his performances through the years was to walk around the set playing cymbals, etc. He was always ready to move!

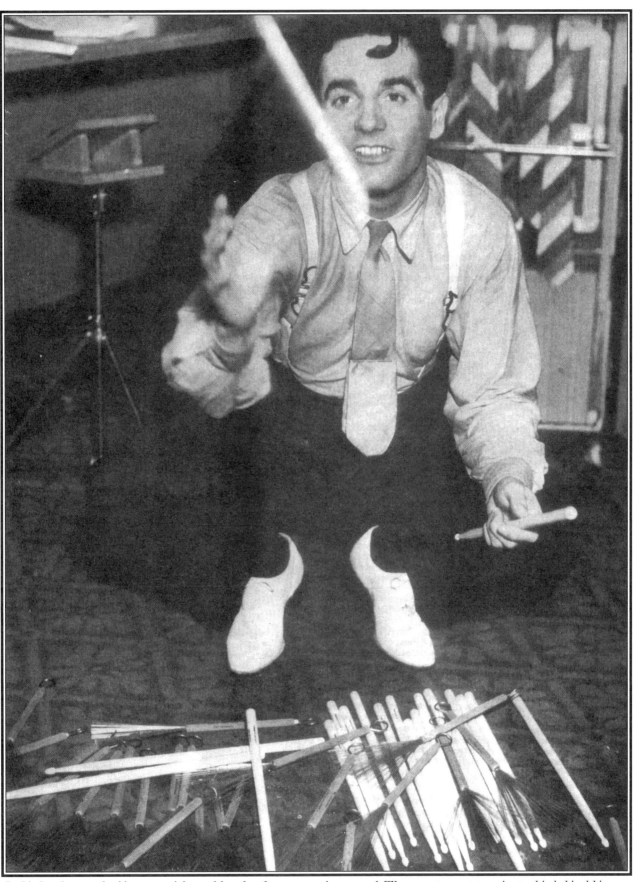

In his hotel room checking out sticks and brushes for a magazine spread. The ever-present practice pad is behind him, and all the sticks were the special "Gene Krupa model" made by Slingerland.

Early rehearsal for the first band. The calfskin heads were already well used. Gene's hand and stick position would be the envy of any drum teacher, then or now.

First "official" portrait of Gene's new orchestra, taken in March, 1938. The vocalist is Jerry Kruger (Hardly remembered at all today, musicologist Gunther Schuller has singled her out as "the link between Billie Holiday and Anita O'Day "and one of the first white singers to emulate Lady Day"). The bandstand-mounted toms were a feature of Gene's early big bands and were used by the sidemen to bang out counter-rhythms while Gene soloed over them. See Carmine Appice's explanation in the "comments" section of this work.

Side view of the man at work, about 1939. The drum seat, engraved with Gene's name, remains a custom model. The angle of the snare drum is a bit less radical, and the floor toms still use a cradle-type holder. The second one, in this shot, is used to hold the band's charts. The drum in the foreground? That's open to speculation.

From the same shoot; one of Gene's favorite facial expressions.

Gene was third-billed to Bob Hope and Shirley Ross in Paramount's 1939 film Some Like it Hot *later retitled* Rhythm Romance. *He proved to be a surprisingly good actor in this comedy trifle, best known for introducing the song* The Lady's in Love with You, *which became a pop standard. There's some good music in the film as well, including* Wire Brush Stomp *and* Blue Rhythm Fantasy. *Among the sidemen, and some are pictured herein, were Sam Musiker on clarinet, Ray Biondi on guitar, San Donahue on tenor sax, Musky Ruffo on alto sax, and possibly Toby Tyler (or Bruce Squires) on trombone. For reasons unknown, star Bob Hope was never happy with this film and had it removed from his every official "filmography." He was happy, however, to give his permission to Paramount a few years ago to release* Rhythm Romance *on VHS video as a part of its Bob Hope collection. More pictures from this session follow on page 47.*

About 1940. Gene loved to fiddle with the artwork on the front bass drum head. Here's the famous "GK," a bit larger and more centered. The cymbal stand on the right has a black, heavy-duty base, and next to that is what appears to be an extra tom that's somehow attached to the mounted tom.

THE BAND THAT SWAMPS THE BOX OFFICE

Gene

KRUPA

AND HIS ORCHESTRA

featuring

Anita O'Day • Roy (Little Jazz) Eldridge • Johnny Desmond

Four times called back to the Panther Room of the Sherman Hotel by Chicago's enthusiastic crowds. Each time cracking a previous box office record. Gene's most recent engagement drew well over 20,000 cash customers.

Get these latest Gene Krupa hit records:
Okeh 6607—Sky Lark, Harlem on Parade
Okeh 6619—Pass The Bounce, Me and My Melinda
Okeh 6635—Fightin' Doug MacArthur
   Night of Nights

Soon To Be Released!
Barrel House Bessie From Basin Street, Deliver Me to Tennessee, Knock Me a Kiss.
Roy (Little Jazz) Eldridge makes his debut here as vocalist with the band.

Now touring the Mid-West crowd centers. Booked solid in six of the mid-west's choicest spots—because he draws the crowds. Check these dates:

Chicago Theater, Chicago, May 1 to 14
Palace Theater, Cleveland, May 15 to 21
Stanley Theater, Pittsburgh, May 22 to 28
Shea Theater, Buffalo, May 29 to June 4
Eastwood Gardens, Detroit, June 5
Cedar Point, Ohio, June 13.

Personal Management
Frank Verniere

Direction
MUSIC CORPORATION OF AMERICA

The 1941 group did become "the band that swamps the box office," due in part to the addition of Anita O'Day and Roy Eldridge. Eldridge, by the way, became the first black artist ever to actually sit in the section of a white big band. Benny Goodman did hire Lionel Hampton and Teddy Wilson a few years earlier for his band, but they were separate "special attractions" in the small groups and not actually a part of the band proper. Roy was in the Krupa band. Gene insisted on it.

Gene, obviously enjoying himself, with the one and only Roy "Little Jazz" Eldridge to his left.

Exuding confidence and movie star charm. Notice the holes in the small mounted tom. Gene made certain that all internal muffling devices were removed from every drum for maximum resonance.

Cymbals were getting larger (though the gong is a new addition) by 1942-1943, and finally, the cymbal holders on the bass drum have shell mounts. The small tom is still hoop-mounted.

A shot from the same job, but look for the old-style "screw-type" anchor used to keep the hi-hat pedal from creeping.

Barbara Stanwyck and Krupa from the 1941 film Ball of Fire. *Stanwyck sang "Drum Boogie" in the movie, though some fans insist it was actually Martha Tilton doing the singing. On the drum set, the bass drum spurs were still hoopmounted, and there's that screw anchor holding the bass drum in place.*

Through much of the 1940s, Gene did his patriotic duty by having a bass drum head that read "Let's Go! Keep 'Em Flyin'." A small part of it is visible in this 1942 photo.

Gene at the Hollywood Palladium in 1943 just before the drug bust, with Roy Eldridge soloing and Tommy Dorsey sitting in. After Gene's release from prison, he would join Dorsey's band for a surprise appearance in New York at the Paramount Theater.

THE DRUG BUST 1943

To this day, if the person on the street is asked to name a drummer, five times out of ten, their answer will be Gene Krupa. It's unfortunate that he is sometimes remembered for the wrong reasons, and much of that has to do with misinformation. The effects of a trumped-up drug case against Gene that took place over 50 years ago still linger. Some of the ridiculous sequences in *The Gene Krupa Story* motion picture didn't help, and even some recent video catalogs, in their blurb about the DVD version of the Krupa story film, have had copy implying that "drugs destroyed him." Many writers through the years have done their best to set the record straight, including D. Russell Connor, John McDonough, Anita O'Day in her autobiography, Burt Korall and Bruce Crowther. Still, we too often hear comments like: "Wasn't he a heroin addict?", "Didn't he die of an overdose?", "He was a real pot-head, wasn't he?". The answer to all those questions was and is "no." Ask anyone who knew him. There wasn't a finer, straighter, more responsible, dedicated or spiritual human being in or out of the jazz world. Mel Tormé could only say "He was an angel." Sure, like a lot of folks, he fooled with the weed in the 1930s and 1940s, but that's as far as it went. After the 1943 drug "scandal," those who knew him well say he never touched it. Scotch was "his thing," they said.

The stories continue to vary in detail about just what happened on January 18, 1943 at the Golden Gate Theater in San Francisco, but what we do know is this: Gene Krupa was arrested on the charge of contributing to the delinquency of a minor, reportedly because he sent his 17-year-old valet to his hotel room for, as they called them then, reefers. The youth, named John Pateakos, testified to the arresting officers that he had been sent to Gene's hotel room to get marijuana cigarettes and that he was to bring them to the theater where Gene was playing. The reefer was in fact in Krupa's overcoat, Gene was put in a paddy wagon, posted $1,000 bond and continued to lead his band until the scheduled May 18 trial.

The press, Walter Winchell in particular, went wild, accusing Krupa of causing juvenile delinquency, popularizing drugs and zoot suits, and the like. Gene, by the way, was able to witness Winchell's eventual downfall and outlived him by a year. He was crucified in the press, and Krupa probably did more harm than good by hiring the well-known criminal defense lawyer Jake Ehrlich, a sworn enemy of the San Francisco District Attorney.

The *true* story later surfaced. Young Pateakos had received his draft notice and wanted to buy Gene a going-way present, and decided that weed would have made a great gift. Federal narcs were tipped off, and they were then set to "get Gene." Ehrlich's advice was that Gene plead guilty to the misdemeanor charge of contributing to the delinquency of a minor, with the opinion being that Gene would get no more than a fine and a suspended sentence. It didn't go down that way.

The publicity was too much. Judge Thomas A. Foley sentenced Gene to 90 days in the county jail. There were more complications along the way, including what loomed as the possibility of a one-to-six year sentence in San Quentin, for "transporting narcotics" (later dropped). Gene did serve 84 days of the original 90-day sentence. His band broke up, his New York furniture and files were thrown out on the street for non-payment of rent, and, as writer Michael Zirpolo so aptly put it in an issue of the *International Association of Jazz Record Collectors' Journal*, "He was now viewed as a jailbird involved with dope and juvenile delinquency. He truly thought his career was over."

For a while it was. But his wife Ethel, whom he divorced in 1941, stood by him (they would remarry in late 1944) and his old boss, Benny Goodman, hired him in December of 1943 for an appearance at the New Yorker Hotel. Gene was still wary of how he would be received in theaters, so it was quite a surprise when he turned up, unbilled and unadvertised, as a part of the Tommy Dorsey Orchestra at the Paramount Theater in New York City in December of 1944. He received a tremendous ovation. "I cried like a baby," Gene said years later. As a postscript, 18 months later, he was cleared of all charges.

The "drug" stigma would remain throughout his career and sometimes take on a life of its own. "I don't think I was exactly a failure," Gene told a television interviewer in the early 1970s, "but on the other hand, I think I could have been a lot more successful in the field. For instance, I just couldn't see doing a cigarette commercial, could you? Not with the stigma I had, don't you see?" Gene's pianist for a time in the 1960s, Dave Frishberg, told writer Bruce Crowther that Gene "couldn't afford to be compromised in any way. He intimated that the police, especially in the small towns, would like nothing better than to bust Gene Krupa and get some local notoriety. I don't even remember seeing Gene take so much as a drink when we were on the job."

Gene Krupa outside the San Francisco County jail just before his release in late summer of 1943.

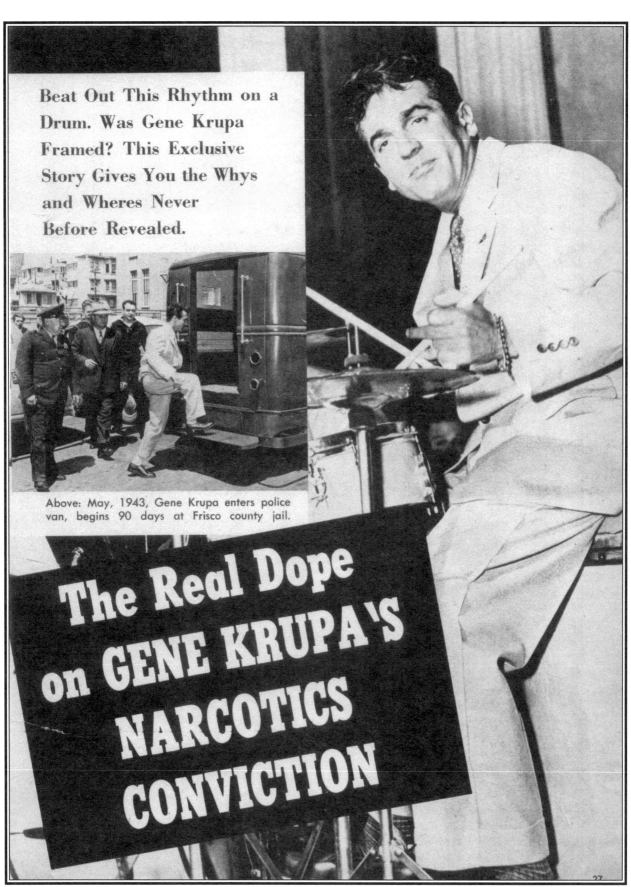

Beat Out This Rhythm on a Drum. Was Gene Krupa Framed? This Exclusive Story Gives You the Whys and Wheres Never Before Revealed.

Above: May, 1943, Gene Krupa enters police van, begins 90 days at Frisco county jail.

The Real Dope on GENE KRUPA'S NARCOTICS CONVICTION

Articles that appeared in sleazy tabloids throughout the years, like this one, helped keep the drug "myth" alive. Actually, this particular story was pretty factual, but the headlines and the small picture of Gene going into the paddy wagon, convey a different story.

THE SECOND BAND 1944-1951

Tommy Dorsey carried a large string section in those days, and Gene loved their sound, having always been a quite knowledgeable classical music fan. When he realized that nightclubs and theaters thankfully welcomed him back after the arrest, he began plans to reform the band. This ensemble would be different. "The Band That Swings With Strings" began rehearsals on June 21, 1944. Krupa often referred to this period as the time of his "Kostelanetz complex." He hired a bunch of singers, a second drummer to play when he felt like conducting, and overall, soft-pedaled anything that might have been really swinging. He couldn't say enough about how much he enjoyed the violin section ("I had dreams of Roy Eldridge playing muted with a fine, soft string background," he was quoted at the time). In retrospect, it's also clear that the concept of a non-threatening dance band with fiddles was a good way to "rehabilitate" the somewhat tarnished Gene Krupa image. By June of the following year the strings were gone, vocalist Anita O'Day rejoined, the swinging resumed, and Gene Krupa became one of the first "name" bandleaders to embrace something called be-bop.

Passing through the second version of the Krupa orchestra were out-and-out modernists like trumpeters Red Rodney, Don Fagerquist, and Al Porcino; trombonists Urbie Green, Tommy Pederson and Frank Rehak; saxophonists Buddy Wise, Charlie Kennedy, Gene Quill and Lenny Hambro, guitarist Dennis Sandole, singers Anita O'Day, Dave Lambert (later of Lambert, Hendricks and Ross) and Buddy Stewart; arrangers Gerry Mulligan, Budd Johnson, Eddie Finckel, Neal Hefti and George Williams. Krupa never made the total transition to modern drumming, but he progressed on his own terms, and whatever he did play, for the most part, fit in. Mel Lewis, for one, thought he was *marvelous* with that band. Those years brought more hit records (Mulligan's *Disc Jockey Jump* and *How High the Moon,* as well as one of the first bop vocal records, entitled *What's This?*), successful recordings by the new Gene Krupa Jazz Trio with pianist Teddy Napoleon and Charlie Ventura, and more motion pictures.

As the decade wore on, the big band business—bop, swing and otherwise—got worse and worse. In 1950, after 12 years on the Columbia record label, Gene left to join RCA Victor, though Victor saw the handwriting on the wall and only released a small number of recordings. With considerable difficulty, he kept his large ensemble going until the end of 1950. In February of 1951, he came back with a 12-piece band, but by the years' end, the Gene Krupa Orchestra was history.

The 1944 "Band That Swings With Strings."

Vocal group, second drummer, fiddle section and kettle drums, all under the supervision of "conductor and maestro" Gene Krupa.

Going to Hollywood on December 23, 1944 via Army B-17.

Some believe that Gene was trying to downplay his "wild man of the drums" image by going the violin route. Pictured here is a kinder, gentler Krupa, if you will.

One of the first engagements of the new band was at the Capitol Theater in New York City in 1944. The line at the box office proves that the arrest had no effect on Gene's popularity.

In 1944, Swank *magazine published "Gene Krupa's Life Story" in booklet form, with plenty of pictures of Gene, the sidemen, and great hype about the new band and his newly revived career. This photo, printed in a two-color process, served as the cover. You can clearly see the holes, top and bottom, in the mounted tom after the removal of the mufflers.*

In action!—from the same booklet with a clear view of the famed "wartime" bass drum head.

This specially made conga drum, in white marine pearl, of course, is proof of one of the few times that Gene asked the Slingerland Drum Company for something special. Note "second drummer" Joe Dale on Gene's drums in the back.

GENE KRUPA
Souvenir Book
BEAUTIFUL STUDIO PORTRAITS, CANDID SHOTS AND BIOGRAPHIES

"The Gene Krupa Life Story" booklet was issued in a slightly different form as the "Gene Krupa Souvenir Book" offered for sale at the band's gigs.

By 1945, the strings were gone and Gene went back to swinging. This is a rather interesting rendering of Gene on the cover of the September, 1945, edition of Band Leaders *magazine.*

Ordinary cameras can't do justice to the work of the King of Hides when he's pounding out "Drumboogie"—all you see is a blur of drumsticks. But, with a special camera set for exposures of 1/25,000 of a second, in the hands of the crack Chicago news photographer Elliott Robinson, you get the exclusive **BAND LEADERS** photos shown on these pages . . . a remarkable stop-action study in facial expression, drumming technique and showmanship.

With a quick switch of drumsticks, the master is off on his solo . . .

Back on the snares, beating out resounding and solid rhythm . . .

Close work on the cymbals brings forth spectacular sound effects . . .

Within the same issue of Band Leaders *was a photo spread of Krupa in action, being photographed by "a special camera set for exposures of 1/25,000 of a second!" Note the spotlights to the side, and the larger cymbals.*

Blowups from the same shoot. Dozens of sticks per week were broken during the Krupa big-band days. Here's the unhappy drummer looking at yet another one in the final frame.

One stick frozen, the other coming in for a crash . . .

Broken drumstick, calling for a split-second halt . . .

*"The Band That Swings With Strings"
made a major motion picture in 1945,
entitled* George White's Scandals. *This is
a scene that was cut from the film, a duet
with organist Ethel Smith. Smith had her
own separate feature in the film.*

*Doing his patriotic duty in behalf of War
Bonds, around 1945.*

The Gene Krupa Jazz Trio had a brief existence within the Tommy Dorsey band when the trio's members were clarinetist Buddy DeFranco and pianist Dodo Marmarosa. The idea was revived at a recording session of March 8, 1945, when the strings and horns couldn't agree on pitch. Gene sent the band home and recorded "Dark Eyes" and "Body and Soul" with tenor saxophonist Charlie Ventura and pianist Teddy Napoleon. Both worked with Krupa, on and off, for years. In these three views of the trio, you can see the smaller drum set he used, with the one cymbal mounted in the center of the bass drum, expressly for the trio. Two more shots from the same trio's performances follow on page 77.

In Front, for a little while, is tenor sax man Charlie Venturo of the Gene Krupa Jazz Trio, who spends much of his time behind the drums, leaving the limelight to the leader. Gene's appearance was an unexpected item in the jazz concert organized by Timmie Rosenkrantz and given a favorable nod above.

The trio was becoming an attraction as a seperate unit, and occasionally did radio broadcasts and concerts on its own. Teddy Napoleon was briefly out of the band when this photo was taken at producer Timmie Rosenkrantz' Town Hall Concert of 1945. Napoleon was replaced at the piano by George Walters, who also recorded several V-Discs with the trio. Walters was not a favorite of the critics, and Napoleon soon returned.

Follow that Music *was an 18-minute film called a "featurette," that starred the Krupa band. What a band it was; with players like Red Rodney, Gerry Mulligan and Charlie Kennedy, all heavily featured in this little romantic comic opus (Gene gets the girl, too). Carolyn Grey was the band's singer then, but that's an actress you see on screen (Grey did do her singing, however).*

Boy What a Girl was a 70-minute feature film made in 1947 with an all-black musical cast that included Slam Stewart and drummer "Big" Sid Catlett. Gene was a special guest star and had some banter with Sid. Here is a very good look at one of the drum sets played by one of the true legends of jazz drumming: Sid Catlett.

Beat the Band, *a feature film from 1947 as well, featured another great organization, with Rodney and Mulligan, plus Marty Napoleon on piano. The reason that cymbal is so high in the air is because Gene eventually stood up and played a solo on it.*

Beat the Band *is fondly remembered by Krupa fans for the "boiler room" scene where Gene beats out the rhythm on the steam pipes when his band was forced to play in the boiler room (see the film to figure out why). The water is starting to steam in this publicity shot.*

In solo from Beat the Band. *Like Buddy Rich, Gene insisted on having his motion picture drum solos filmed and recorded "live" as often as possible. The miming just looked too phony.*

In case there were any questions, here's a full-fledged bebopper on the cover of Metronome, *September, 1948.*

Everybody's still boppin' about a year later. That's singer Dolores Hawkins.

Here's Gene And Bands When He First Started As Leader

Chicago—Gene Krupa, who got his start in the music business some 20 years ago, became known as one of the great drummers in jazz with Benny Goodman, then went out on his own as a leader, above is shown with two of his earliest bands. First shot was taken late in 1937, with Gene looking as if he hadn't even started shaving yet. You might recognize Remo Biondi, guitarist, who returned to the band recently, Vido Musso, at the left of the sax section, and vocalist Jerry Kruger. Second pic was taken on a movie set, two years later. Note the same music stands, except a drum now has been added to the piano. Here's the lineup: piano—Milt Raskin; guitar—Biondi; saxes—Sam Musiker, Musky Ruffo, Bob Snyder, and Sam Donahue, trumpets —Jack Mootz, Ray Cameron, and Dick Lotter; trombones —Bruce Squires, Al Sherman, and Dalton Rizzotto, Bassist is Horace Rollins. The drummer you know.

PROFILING THE PLAYERS
Members Of Krupa Crew Tell Their Lives, Interests

LENNY HAMBRO (alto sax & clarinet). Senior member of the band, having been with Gene longer than any other sideman. A native and resident of New York City, he's 26 years of age. Has played with the bands of Bobby Byrne and Billy Butterfield. His hobby is swimming. Favorite record is Duke Ellington's *Warm Valley,* mainly because of the work thereon of Johnny Hodges. Is single.

BILL DAVIS (alto sax). Hailing and, down south, played with the *Auburn Knights and Al Coleman's orchestra. His hobby is collecting records, favorite among them being Woody Herman's Early Autumn. Is single.*

RAY DAVIDSON (baritone sax). Another Texan, Ray's home is in Carthage. He's 28 and has played with the bands of Don Ragon, Buddy Ryland, and Rocky Hampton. Has three favorite records, being unable to single out

He's worked with Bob Chester, Kay Kyser, and several lesser name bands. Swimming is listed as his hobby with "zoo keeper" as alternate. Dizzy's Manteca is his favorite disc. Is married and has a 2-year-old daughter.

FERN CARON (trumpet). Comes from up Lewiston, Maine, way and is 29 years old. Formerly played with Sam Donahue, Les Brown, Billy Butterfield, Charlie Ventura, Teddy Powell, Ruby Newman, Charlie Barnet, and Ray Anthony. Is married and has a 3½-year-old daughter.

GENE MULLINS (trombone). From Auburn, Ala., Gene is 21-years-old, and Gene's is his first major band association. Is a bookworm, spending as much spare time as possible reading. *Mathis der Maler* by Paul Hindemith is his favorite recording. Is single.

IRBY GREEN (trombone). Another lad from the southland, Irby's hometown is Mobile, Ala. He's

Downs 3 To Brooklyn

New York—The Evelyn Downs trio has gone into the Park Terrace, Brooklyn, for a six months stay. Present lineup of the trio is Dorothy McLean, guitar; Helen Kova, accordion, and Evelyn Downs, Hammond organ.

photographer. In the waxworks, he prefers anything by Jimmy Blanton. Had his own band and worked with Lee Williams, Sammy Fletcher, and Bob McGrew. Is Single.

NORMAN SCHNELL (piano). From Cranbury, N. J., Norm is 25 and formerly worked with the band of Sammy Fletcher. *Early Autumn* by Woody is his fave disc and he lists "bird watcher" as his hobby. Is single.

REMO BIONDI (guitar). Like Krupa, Remo is from Chicago. His hobby is cartooning and the favorite record of this 42-year-old

Goodman Back With Columbia

New York—Benny Goodman has returned to Columbia records, the label he left to go to Capitol almost three years ago. Columbia has signed him to a three-year contract under which he'll cut both longhair and pop sides.

Deal also gives Columbia rights to records made of Goodman's 1938 concert at Carnegie hall, which spot many of the top jazzmen of the late '30s. These will be transferred to two 12-inch LPs and will be issued, according to a Columbia spokesman, "within the near future."

Goodman's contract with Capitol still had several months to go. It's understood it was wound up by mutual agreement. This is Benny's second term with Columbia. He also

The band business was quickly going downhill by 1950, but Gene Krupa was one of the few leaders still hanging in there. Down Beat *magazine was kind enough to give the band some "shot-in-the-arm" publicity by publishing a Krupa tribute in its August 25, 1950 issue. Less than a year later, the band would be history.*

Anita O'Day became a star in the Krupa band during her two tenures with the group (1941 to 1943, and again 1945). Anita was the only Krupa band alumnus to appear in The Gene Krupa Story. *They remained dear friends for life.*

Still hanging in there by late 1950.

THE 1950s

The 1950s were good times for Gene. Freed of the economic albatross of a big band, Gene reformed his jazz trio with Charlie Ventura and Teddy Napoleon, joined Norman Granz' Jazz at the Philharmonic troupe, and traveled all over the world with the legendary artists that comprised the JATP organization. In April of 1952, the Gene Krupa Jazz Trio became the first American jazz group in history to tour Japan, and in October, he took part in what later became one of the most famous recording sessions in drum history, *The Drum Battle*, with Buddy Rich. There were other highlights: He took over leadership of the Benny Goodman band in 1953 when Goodman pulled out of what could have been a landmark tour with Louis Armstrong; took part in the filming of *The Glenn Miller Story* and *The Benny Goodman Story*; formed a drum school in New York City with fellow drummer Cozy Cole; made dozens of network television appearances; had a fine recording contract with Verve Records; and by the end of the decade became one of the very few artists in the history of jazz to have a feature film made about their life.

As a drummer, though no longer at the vanguard of innovation, Gene Krupa was more musical than ever, and began exploring the colors and the possibilities of the cymbals as well as the drums. With the addition of more modern players to his groups through the decade—including reedmen Eddie Shu and Eddie Wasserman, pianists Dave McKenna, Ronnie Ball and Bobby Scott, and bassists John Drew, Jimmy Gannon and Whitey Mitchell—Gene was able to evolve musically and comfortably within his own style. A heart attack in 1960 slowed him down somewhat, but as he was later to say, it forced him to think about music more with his *head* than his arms.

In the basement of his Yonkers, New York, home in 1951, studying percussion with New York Philharmonic tympanist Saul Goodman.

Krupa Re-Forms Trio; Ventura Joins

Barnet Band Has People Dancing In Portland Date

By TED HALLOCK

Portland, Ore.—The Mab's back and nobody's got him. Charlie Barnet has a new 17-piece band. It is neither *Cu-Ba* nor *Tappin' at the Tappa*. It's nothing like the Tiny Kahn-Buddy Stewart band and less like the Cliff Leeman-Bus Etri band. It isn't 1939 or 1949. It is definitely, however, more fish than foul.

In a musical world of likening styles and artists to other styles and artists, one could best compare Charlie's new crew to the group which recorded for black label Decca in 1944, etching *West End Blues*, *Skyline*, and other gems. It is definitely a swinging swing band, playing for dancing (though only 750 showed up during Barnet's Jantzen Beach one-niter here).

Few New Tunes

The new band, formed 10 days before its December Portland date, smacked of the period during which its book (Charlie has his choice of so many) was introduced. Very few new tunes were played. Possibly Barnet hit the road only for loot, using pickup men; possibly to sample the new (alleged) trend to Goodman-type big band jazz.

The date was reminiscent of pre-bop dances; dancers made as much sense (as an audience) as the orchestra did musically. Whether you're pro or con-jitterbug, you must concede they were a manifestation of healthier times. Barnet's date saw plenty of them, engaged in active admiration of the obvious beat, surrounded by throngs of terpsichoreah connoisseurs.

The kids, like old times, had a helluva fine evening. They didn't have to worry about intricate rhythms, a complex melodic line, dissonant extended and altered chords, and other aspects of atonal neurosis.

Few Soloists

lepigue, and Manny Albam.

Charlie has introduced a sextet within the band (Barnet, Markham, Harrington, Smith, Sarmento, and Eddie Bert) with which he may work in the near future, though the big band will one-night in L.A. and the southwest for a few months. The success of this venture tells the tale.

Charlie says, somewhat cryptically: "With business so uncertain now, I'll just coast along until something better comes along." With Barnet's record, the present band is the best thing to come along in a long while.

He adds, "People today don't know how to dance. There seems to be a barrier between bands and the people. The 'Golden Era' when Goodman was at his peak was a time when music and the dancing public were in perfect harmony. This is a subject I am going to write an article on . . . soon."

From the reaction of those dancers present, he can save his ink and sand.

Music People Named In Bankhead Episode

New York—Several jazz personalities were mentioned during the two weeks of testimony at the trial of Tallulah Bankhead's former secretary, Mrs. Evy-cocaine. None of this evidence was substantiated and Moritt wound up earning two citations for contempt of court for the way he handled the case.

Gypsy Miss

Hollywood—Now known only under the moniker "Miss Antonina," this attractive chick formerly sang as Charlene Bartley with the band of Al Donahue. However, Al is now in Bermuda, where he appeared New Year's Eve at the Bermudiana hotel, and Miss A. is out doing a single. She can be heard on Donahue's newest release, *Gypsy Magic*, from which the idea for her costume in this photo may have stemmed.

Don Elliott Rehearses Big Band

New York—Don Elliott, triple-threat soloist most recently heard with Teddy Wilson at the Embers, has been rehearsing a big band.

The outfit comprises six brass, five reeds, three rhythm, and a vocal group with Joan Cavanaugh. Elliott plays mellophone voiced with the brass, and vibes with a combo within the band. He also sings.

At presstime auditions were being conducted, using arrangements by Ralph Burns and Gil Evans. Organization on a permanent basis depended on the corralling of the necessary capital.

Contino Freed; Plans To Wed, Then Enlist

Hollywood—Dick Contino, young accordionist whose career as a high-salaried nitery and stage performer was interrupted by his conviction on a draft evasion charge, was released from the federal prison at McNeil Island after serving 4½ months.

The youngster, who was earning as high as $4,000 a week, went AWOL from an induction center in what those close to him have always held to have been a state of emotional confusion. A few days later he gave himself up and pleaded guilty.

His original sentence of six months was reduced because of good behavior and his complete cooperation with prison authorities. Contino spent Christmas with his parents at his home in Glendale, a Los Angeles suburb. He told friends he was going to get married and then apply for enlistment. He still faces a $10,000 fine.

New York—The Gene Krupa trio has been revived.

Krupa, Charlie Ventura, and Teddy Napoleon, famed unit within a band of the late '40s, broke in with a three-day date at Ventura's Open House on Jan. 16, then opened at the State theater, Hartford.

A series of TV, radio, and theater dates has been set up for the group already, with plenty of jazz location stands available if Krupa wants to play them.

This puts to an end the rumors that Gene, following his *JATP* hegira, would (1) reorganize his big band or (2) join the Big Four.

Main incentive behind the reunion of the threesome after a five-year separation, says Krupa, is the great reception given the recent issuance of the trio's Mercury LP, cut at a *JATP* session in Los Angeles in 1946.

Arnold Ross 3 To Back Horne On Europe Trip

Hollywood—Pianist Arnold Ross headlines the new trio put together here which will accompany Lena Horne on her forthcoming tour, a jaunt starting at Miami, Fla., on Jan. 23 and including a six-month tour of Europe.

Bassist Joe Benjamin, who has worked with instrumental groups backing the singer at various times in the past, came out from New York to rejoin, and a Local 47 drummer, not set at deadline, was to be added here.

Miss Horne, her husband Lennie Hayton, who will conduct house

The Down Beat *headline of February 8, 1952, says it all.*

In April of 1952, The Gene Krupa Jazz Trio, with Charlie Ventura (playing bass sax here) and pianist Teddy Napoleon, became the first American jazz group to tour Japan, and recorded for Japanese Victor while there. According to the members of the trio, they were treated like royalty, were front-page news, and given "ticker-tape" parades wherever they went.

GENE KRUPA
ON JAPAN

If an American jazz musician wants a boost in ego, and isn't afraid of hard work, let him go to Japan for a few weeks.

Jap people, at least the thousands we encountered who appear to be interested in American jazz, are the most enthusiastic and responsive of any I've come across in all my travels.

By American standards, we were greeted like native heroes. I can't begin to estimate the size of the crowd that greeted us at the Tokyo airport. It was huge. They were cheering us before we'd even set up a cymbal in Japan. Geisha girls presented us with more flowers at the airport than you'll find in the Botanical Gardens. Then, to our complete surprise—and slight embarrassment—the powers that be put each of us in a touring car and gave us a ticker-tape parade welcome up the main streets of Tokyo. They couldn't have given us a better reception if we were "The MacArthur Trio."

The enthusiasm was the same at each and every performance, be it theater or night club, Tokyo, Yokohama or Osaki. None of us is cold-hearted enough to pass over such demonstrations or to say we disliked such treatment. However, there are some other items that impressed me equally as much. Perhaps it was the unexpected angle.

For instance, the pit orchestra at the Nichigeki, Tokyo's largest

theater, both surprised and thrilled me. Containing upwards o thirty pieces, the band, all Japanese of course, had conceptio and intonation such as we'd hardly expected to find over ther The instrumentation was typical of that found in bands o similar size in the states. The selections, for the most part, als were pop American tunes. Probably through a combination o being perfectionists in whatever they undertake, and expert imita tors, tne Jap musicians turn in an excellent performance.

Then, too, there are the singers who appeared with the band A girl sang an American song, I believe it was *Tennessee Waltz*, s much like Patti Page, it would be hard to tell the difference were not for the locale. A Jap youth sang *Deep Purple* exactly lik Billy Eckstine.

In both cases when the artists left the stage and passed u in the wings, we offered our congratulations on their fine voc efforts. Both times it fell on deaf ears. The singers couldn't under stand a word of English. Yet, having studied the phonograp records of the American artists, they'd learned them phoneticall to give a perfect performance. Similar incidents occurred man times after that during our tour.

The Geisha girls still play the traditional one-stringed Japanes instruments, so familiar in Nipponese art, in the presentation o their dances, but I saw no other evidence of those old-time music heirlooms.

I did run across plenty of small jazz groups, many with ex cellent conceptions of various styles. Again they learn a lot phonet cally via discs, but don't we all?

Record-wise, in the jazz field, I found the Japanese very muc up on their Kenton, Stan Getz, Louis Armstrong, George Shearin and, I'm happy to say, Charlie Ventura and myself.

The Japanese people were very gracious, despite what you rea in the papers about the May Day demonstrations. We were in th

(Continued on page 31

Music Trade *magazine feature on the trio's trip to Japan. These photos were actually taken during Gene's concerts there.*

While with Jazz at the Philharmonic, three giants had a chance to come together backstage. This is Gene, Buddy Rich and Max Roach.

Also backstage at Jazz at the Philharmonic, some years earlier (1947), Gene and Buddy with one of their absolute favorites, "Papa" Jo Jones.

The JATP musical situations were varied, and a number of different horn players were used to fill out the Krupa Trio. This one, with Flip Phillips on tenor saxophone and Teddy Napoleon on piano, could have been great, but lasted only about a month, during a July 1952 tour of Sweden.

Back in the States in 1953, backing Benny Carter on alto saxophone. The ever-present spotlights were still there on Gene's kit, but at long last, the drum set had been modernized with all shell-mount hardware, an up-to-date bass drum anchor, and a nice-sized ride cymbal.

With Benny Goodman and Teddy Wilson prior to the start of the Goodman/Louis Armstrong tour that Goodman eventually abandoned. Stories abound about why Benny left, with many maintaining he just couldn't stand being out-played and less loved by audiences than Armstrong. Krupa eventually took over leadership of the Goodman band and the tour was said to be pretty successful. Gene was experimenting with some larger-sized ride cymbals during this decade, and at times may have gone to a 24-inch or even 26-inch model.

Backstage with the JATP stars in the early 1950s. (Left to right) Flip Phillips, Oscar Peterson, Norman Granz, Gene, and Kai Winding.

One of the most famous drum recordings ever made, The Drum Battle, *in 1952.*

SET 2

THE OSCAR PETERSON
TRIO

Oscar Peterson, piano
Ray Brown, bass
Barney Kessel, guitar

*   *   *

THE GENE KRUPA TRIO

Gene Krupa, drum
Hank Jones, piano
Willie Smith, alto saxophone

*   *   *

ELLA FITZGERALD

accompanied by Hank Jones

*   *   *

FINALE

Part of the JATP program sold at Norman Granz concerts. This Krupa trio with Willie Smith and Hank Jones was one of the strongest, and it's the group heard the Drum Battle *album.*

1954 at the Last Frontier Hotel lounge in Las Vegas with bassist John Drew and Eddie Shu on saxophone. Not pictured is Bobby Scott on piano. Drew, from England, was the first bassist ever in the small group, finally making the trio a quartet.

A great shot of the Slingerlands at the same engagement. Look at the size of that ride cymbal! The engraving on the top hoop of the mounted tom—"Slingerland Radio King"— is visible.

Rare cover to the Japanese Victor 45 rpm extended play recording made by the reconstituted Jazz Trio during their April, 1952 visit to Japan. These wonderful sides were never formally issued in the United States, but remain among the best recordings the trio ever made.

The group that Bobby Scott spoke so highly of in his foreword, comprised of (right to left) Scott, bassist Whitey Mitchell, Gene and Eddie Shu, making like The Four Aces at the State Theatre in Hartford, Connecticut.
(Photo courtesy of Whitey Mitchell.)

The 1954 motion picture, The Glenn Miller Story, *featured a mini-drum duel between Gene and Cozy Cole during a Louis Armstrong "jam session" scene. Cole was Armstrong's drummer at that time, and these are Cozy's drums, with the snare drum looking very much like a Gretsch-Gladstone model. This movie did very well at the box office and inspired the making of* The Benny Goodman Story *a year later.*

Gone Man of the Week: Gum-chewing Gene Krupa frantically pounds the drums and cymbal in a solo during the filming of the life story of band leader Glenn Miller, killed in the war.

Another shot of Gene behind Cozy Cole's drums during the filming of The Glenn Miller Story.

The Miller film also served as the perfect "publicity kickoff" for the opening of The Krupa/Cole Drum School in 1954. Cole had a big record hit with Topsy Part 2 *in 1959, was on the road touring and was rarely at the school, and Krupa admitted that he didn't have much patience for teaching. The school did well, and its doors stayed open until the early 1960s.*

In March of 1954, two great drummers and good friends teamed up to open a drum school. This was a double-page spread ad that appeared in Downbeat *magazine, complete with best wishes from Slingerland and Zildjian. On paper, the idea made sense, in that Gene and Cozy were frequently working at the Metropole Café in New York city at the time. Gene publicized it whenever he could, and even mentioned the school on television several times. It did very, very well but eventually closed in the early 1960s as the "founders" just weren't able to be there very much.*

The full poster announcing the opening of the Krupa/Cole drum school.

The Benny Goodman Story *captured little of the magic, or the box office, of* The Glenn Miller Story, *due to a hackneyed plot and less than credible acting. It did give great, on-screen exposure to a number of great players, including pianist Teddy Wilson, pictured here with Krupa and star Steve Allen. Wilson always credited the film for reviving his touring career.*

Publicity shot from The Benny Goodman Story, *looking at the crowds from the point of view of the drummer.*

The full band in The Benny Goodman Story *re-creating swing's beginning at the Palomar Ballroom in Los Angeles. Goodman himself, who had control over the music and the musicians in the film, made some interesting choices of musicians for this group, including saxophonist Stan Getz (far right), who had played with Benny for about a year in 1945, and trumpeter Buck Clayton (center trumpet), who never played with Goodman's bands.*

At one of the late-1950s Timex All Star Jazz Spectaculars on television, with (left to right) Steve Allen, Woody Herman and Jack Teagarden in the background.

Another 1950s television get together on CBS-TV with Mel Tormé, on a snare drum and Krupa playing quite a small drum set (the "GK" bass head is still on there).

Going at it with gusto during a Jazz at the Philharmonic tour of Germany in 1959, playing Dave Bailey's drums. Bailey was playing with Gerry Mulligan's group, also on the tour.

GENE KRUPA

Three views (pp.116, 117, 118) of Gene Krupa at the end of the decade (the autographed one was his "official" publicity photo back then) show a contented, elder statesman of the drums. He was particularly proud of late 1950s group, which featured Eddie Wasserman on saxophone, clarinet and flute (Eddie's on the far right playing flute in a shot taken at Chicago's London House night club); Lennie Tristano student Ronnie Ball on piano; and bassist Jimmy Gannon.

The Gene Krupa Story

The 1959 Columbia Pictures film, "The Gene Krupa Story," is a pretty odd entry in the legendary drummer's history. The music was terrific, with an all-star orchestra that included the cream of Hollywood studio personnel, including trumpeters Peter Candoli and Conrad Gozzo, reedmen Dave Pell and Benny Carter, Jimmy Rowles and Jess Stacy on piano, Barney Kessel on guitar, and the man himself—along with Shelly Manne playing the part of Dave Tough—on drums. Gene rarely sounded better. It may have been for economic reasons, but most of artists who played such an important part in Gene's career, like Benny Goodman, Roy Eldridge and Charlie Ventura, were simply ignored, though Red Nichols and Anita O'Day did make cameos. Eldridge was said to be quite miffed at being left out. Likewise, his greatest musical hits were not included, in favor of tunes like "Cherokee" and "Indiana." Leith Stevens was credited with adapted and composing the music. The soundtrack album was issued on the Verve Celebrity Series label in 1960 and has not yet found its way to commercial compact disc release.

Those in charge of the actual filming were producer Phillip A. Waxman and director Don Weis, whose credentials were mostly in the B-picture area. Waxman was responsible for the 1951 trifle with John Barrymore, Jr., *The Big Night;* and Weis was later known for *Pajama Party* and, *The Sparing Munster's Revenge.* Quite a legacy. Screenwriter and associate producer Orin Jannings was an A-player, known for his screenplay for the 1958 war drama, *A Time to Love and a Time to Die*, but he had absolutely no affinity with the lives or words of jazz musicians. It was the opinion of the late Moses Wax, who published the film industry publication *Film Bulletin*, that *The Gene Krupa Story* was "ground out quickly and cheaply in black and white as drive-in teen fodder, complete with the casting of teen heartthrobs Sal Mineo and James Darren."

Mineo, a pretty fair drummer himself who idolized Gene, did one of the finest film miming jobs anywhere, playing to Krupa's soundtrack drumming, and the film does have a certain sincere charm. Looking carefully, one of the first instances of an on-screen drum company endorsement comes in the scene where a down-and-out Gene Krupa is playing in a strip club! A small "Slingerland" logo makes an appearance on the bass drum head.

The man himself may have been a bit embarrassed by the whole result, and unlike Benny Goodman's involvement in *The Benny Goodman Story*, Gene seems to have relinquished any rights over the control of how his life was "interpreted." Some of his promotional efforts in behalf of the film, including a "mystery guest" segment with Sal Mineo on television's *I've Got a Secret*, show his discomfort talking about the film.

Years later, Krupa would sometimes introduce himself as "Sal Mineo" during personal appearances, but in a moment of seriousness about the film, he said that he thought "the movie could have been better. They had to pretty everything up, you know. And I think they did it the way they thought I would have liked it to have been. But if they merely did it the way it was, it could have been a great picture."

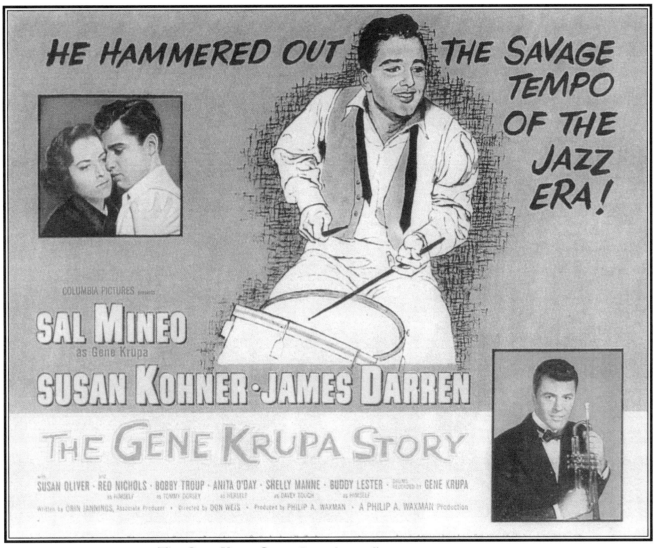

Movie theater lobby card for The Gene Krupa Story. *Love that tagline.*

Susan Kohner, who portrayed Gene's girlfriend (later wife) Ethel and Sal Mineo.

Publicity still of Mineo as Krupa in one of the film's early jam session scenes. That's Bobby Troup on trombone portraying Tommy Dorsey and trumpeter Red Nichols playing himself. After viewing the film, one critic wrote that in the movie, "Red Nichols looked not one day older than he actually was." (Red was about 55 years old at this time and was supposed to be portraying a 20-year-old!)

Sal at the drums giving his best Krupa impersonation.

Entre l'amour qui apaise le cœur et celui qui l'affole,
Gene Krupa hésita longtemps, dans sa fureur de vivre...

Ce jour-là, le jeune Gene Krupa avait le cœur en fête. Il rapportait chez ses parents plusieurs tambours — toute une batterie — qu'il avait pu racheter à bon prix. Il l'installa dans la salle à manger. Il se préparait à jouer quand sa mère entra dans la pièce, accompagnée de son frère. La soudaine tristesse de son visage révélait qu'elle redoutait quelque chose.

Presque aussitôt, le père de Gene arriva. Il demanda à son fils s'il ne lui suffisait pas de frapper du matin au soir sur des casseroles. Il lui reprocha de ne pas chercher de travail alors qu'à son âge, dix-huit ans, la plupart de ses amis travaillaient. Et il lui rappela qu'il

ROLAND FOUGERES VOUS RACONTE LE FILM DE DON WEIS

LA VIE ARDENTE DE GENE KRUPA

(THE GENE KRUPA STORY)

Comme le vieil homme lui intimait l'or-

The French loved jazz and the French loved Sal Mineo. They devoted two gigantic pages to the release of The Gene Krupa Story in an oversized magazine (it actually measured 10 by 14 inches) called Cine' Tele-Revue. Photo to the left is Mineo and Kohner, to the right is Mineo and Yvonne Craig, later known as television's "Bat Girl."

Gene se sentait bien, lui aussi, quand il parlait à Ethel.   Lorsqu'il se déchaînait, Gene semblait possédé par le rythme.

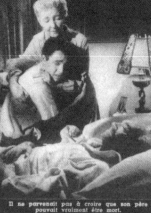

Il ne parvenait pas à croire que son père pouvait vraiment être mort.

avidité. Comme il semblait hésiter à la prendre dans ses bras, elle arracha la chaîne qu'il portait au cou et elle la laissa glisser dans son décolleté qu'elle avait généreux.

— Si tu la veux, il faudra la prendre toi-même, petit tambour, dit-elle en riant.

Gene n'avait jamais beaucoup songé aux filles, parce que, toujours, il était accompagné par l'idée que son père le destinait à la prêtrise. Il resta un moment, les bras ballants, devant Gloria qui éclata d'un rire sonore. Alors, il la saisit, la souleva, jambes en l'air et la tête dirigée vers le sol. Il fit ainsi tomber, de son corsage, dans l'herbe, la chaîne qu'elle lui avait prise. Puis, sans se retourner, il s'en fut retrouver Ethel.

Ce fut un soir en rentrant de la cave, les oreilles encore pleines du rythme de ses tambours, qu'il trouva les siens agenouillés devant le lit du père en pleurant. Le vieillard était mort tandis qu'il jouait, dans la cave, sa musique maudite. Il se jeta sur le lit. Il ne parvenait pas à croire que son père pouvait vraiment être mort.

Dès le lendemain, il partit pour le séminaire. Il sentait que, pour se libérer du sentiment de culpabilité qui l'obsédait, il n'y avait qu'un moyen : devenir prêtre comme le souhaitait son père. Durant les dix mois qu'il passa au séminaire, avant les vacances, il s'efforça de prier et de suivre tous les offices avec ferveur mais, derrière la musique sacrée, à l'église, il lui semblait entendre un rythme de tambour et, la nuit, il faisait des rêves à la fois tristes et exaltants, au cours desquels il frappait sur d'innombrables tambours qui l'entouraient en se multipliant.

Honnêtement, il avoua au directeur du séminaire qu'il ne se croyait pas fait, malgré tous ses efforts, pour la prêtrise. Le directeur lui conseilla d'attendre la

avec surprise entrer dans la cave en compagnie de son frère. Elle lui dit qu'elle voulait voir pourquoi il avait renoncé à devenir prêtre. Il essaya de lui expliquer ce que représentait pour lui ce rythme qu'il tirait de ses tambours. Mais elle ne voyait que la cave enfumée, l'alcool interdit sur les tables, les filles qui dansaient en épousant fidèlement de leur corps les mouvements de leur cavalier. Elle ne trouvait, dans cette cave, que l'image du péché. Les dernières paroles qu'elle dit à Gene avant de le quitter sonnèrent à ses oreilles comme une malédiction.

Ce fut cette nuit-là qu'il forma le projet de partir à New York. Pour devenir célèbre et pour prouver à sa mère qu'il avait eu raison. Il en parla à Ethel ; elle l'encouragea dans cette idée ; elle croyait en lui, en Eddie, en elle-même, en ce qu'ils représentaient avec leur jeunesse et leurs espoirs. Eddie, plus raisonnable, se montra plus réticent. Il redoutait la grande ville où ils ne seraient plus rien. Mais il finit par se laisser convaincre.

Ils débarquèrent à New York par un petit matin gris. Le spectacle de la grande ville remplit Gene d'enthousiasme. Il était pressé de prendre à bras-le-corps cette cité grouillante où naissaient les gloires. Mais, jour après jour, ils parcoururent en vain, Eddie et lui, les impresarii et les directeurs de cabarets. Parfois, on leur autorisait une audition, mais, nulle part, on ne voulait de leur musique. Bientôt, ils atteignirent le fond de leurs économies. Pourtant, ils avaient modéré leurs dépenses. Malgré l'interdiction que leur en faisait le règlement de l'hôtel, Ethel cuisinait dans leur chambre. Lorsqu'elle n'eut plus d'argent, elle trouva une place de téléphoniste et ce fut elle qui les nourrit. Ils en étaient bien un peu gênés, mais, par lâcheté, ils omettaient d'en parler à Ethel. Ils se répétaient entre eux qu'elle

turne, brillant de ses millions de lumières. Ce spectacle fascina Gene. Il lui sembla que cette ville allait lui appartenir. Lorsque Red Nichols, Tommy Dorsey et leurs amis se préparèrent à interpréter un morceau, il eut l'audace, parce qu'il avait vu New York à ses pieds, de prendre à la batterie la place de Davey. Voyant que les musiciens, qui portaient les noms les plus célèbres du jazz de cette époque, considéraient avec étonnement le jeune inconnu qu'il était et ne se décidaient pas à entamer leur morceau, il se lança dans un étourdissant solo. Bientôt, tous les invités se pressèrent autour de lui. Un peu à l'écart, Dorissa fermait les yeux, la bouche un peu entrouverte, comme si elle se trouvait au bord de l'extase. Red Nichols se joignit à lui, puis Tommy Dorsey et les autres suivirent.

A la fin de la soirée, Tommy Dorsey l'avait engagé dans son orchestre. Il l'annonça triomphalement à Ethel et à Eddie. Peu de temps après, il parvenait à y faire entrer Eddie.

Ethel était heureuse de son succès. Pourtant, il lui arrivait souvent de regretter les jours passés où ils avaient à peine de quoi s'acheter à manger. Alors, Gene lui appartenait. Maintenant, il lui faisait faux-bond à la plupart de leurs rendez-vous. Elle le lui pardonnait parce que, s'il lui manquait, c'était toujours pour voir des gens importants pour sa carrière, mais elle se demandait souvent s'il l'aimait autant qu'elle l'aimait.

Pour le soir de son anniversaire, il lui promit de refuser tous les autres rendez-vous, même si c'était avec le président des Etats-Unis. Ce soir-là, il devait accompagner, avec l'orchestre, une chanson qu'enregistrait Dorissa. Il promit à Ethel de la rejoindre aussitôt après.

L'enregistrement commença mal. Dorissa était nerveuse. Elle prétendit que, si rien n'allait, c'était à cause de cette batterie qui faisait un vacarme in-

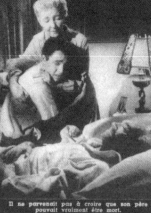

Dans la cave d'autrefois, il retrouva Eddie et Ethel.

vait que c'était à cause d'Ethel. Il vit cette dernière de moins en moins. Ses succès et Dorissa ne lui en laissaient pas le temps. Finalement pourtant, il l'emmena dans un night-club. C'était la première fois qu'il sortait avec elle depuis longtemps. Mais il y rencontra des amis célèbres. Il se laissa entraîner. Il s'excusa auprès d'Ethel en lui assurant que, si ce n'était pas pour sa carrière, il n'agirait pas de la sorte. Elle partit avec

Detailed description of the movie in French and a montage of some memorable film moments.

126

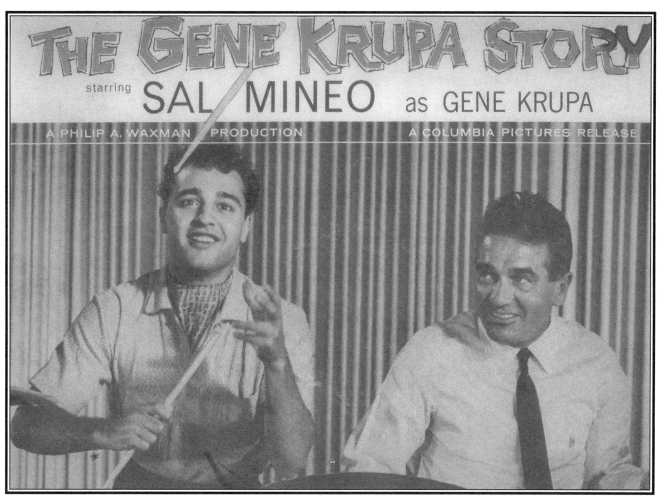

Cover to the soundtrack album.

On the Columbia Pictures' soundstage in Hollywood, recording the drum parts for the film. Notice the bent cymbal on Gene's left. Gene kept playing that for years and didn't care what it looked like. He just loved the sound.

THE 1960s

"You can't fly at a fast pace forever," Gene told *Down Beat* magazine in 1962. "A time comes when you stop and take stock. After my heart attack in November of 1960, I came to the realization that, considering my situation and the condition of the music business, I would do well to cool a bit and concentrate on several things I had been putting off for years."

His slow down didn't last long. In June of 1961, he recorded *Classics in Percussion*, later known as *Gene Krupa: Percussion King*, a series of semi-symphonic pieces for jazz orchestra and large percussion section arranged by George Williams. In November, he took part in the television special *Chicago and All That Jazz*, in 1962 teamed up with Buddy Rich for their third get-together that was called *Burnin' Beat*, in 1963 recorded for RCA Victor with a reassembled Goodman quartet. Iin the summer, Gene put his big band together again for a series of fun dates at Disneyland.

The Gene Krupa Quartet was given a shot in the arm musically when saxophonist Charlie Ventura returned to the group, with featured billing, in late 1963. The following year, they toured Mexico and Japan. In 1965, with Carmen Leggio playing saxophone in place of Ventura, the quartet visited South America; in 1966, with multi-instrumentalist Eddie Shu back in the group, they toured Israel. There were dozens of appearances on national television (one memorable one took place with Buddy Rich on the *Sammy Davis, Jr. Show* in 1966), and regular club appearances in venues he had been working for years, including Chicago's London House, Atlantic City's Steel Pier, New York City's Metropole Café, Detroit's Baker's Keyboard Lounge, San Francisco's Hong Kong Bar, and Al Hirt's nightclub in New Orleans.

After playing some dates in the summer of 1967, Gene Krupa decided that he had it and announced his retirement. Tired of the road after almost 40 years and beset by health problems, he said, "I feel too lousy to play and I know I must sound lousy." For almost two years, he did nothing but play with his kids, practice, read, watch television and coach his local baseball team.

At the filming of the Chicago and All That Jazz, *"Dupont Show of the Week" television special of November, 1961. Gene was reunited with musical friends from his early Chicago days, all pictured: (Front, left to right) Jimmy McPartland on cornet, Jack Teagarden on trombone, Bud Freeman on tenor sax, and Pee Wee Russell on clarinet. That's Eddie Condon on guitar and Bob Haggart on bass in the rear. Look at the size of that ride cymbal and what appears to be a 16 by 18 inch floor tom. Looking carefully, there's a "Slingerland" logo that was "whited out" for television at the top of the bass drum head.*

Sunday supplement to the New York Daily News *announcing an appearance at a newspaper-sponsored jazz fest. That's Gene's new wife Pat to the left, and Gene is holding a copy of the then-just-released* Classics in Percussion *LP.*

Shelly Manne, Gene and Louis Bellson in the middle of Dodger Stadium for a 1962 guest shot on a summer replacement television program called The Lively Ones *hosted by Vic Damone. This memorable sequence had each one of the greats doing battle on the actual ball field, then running around the place banging on literally hundreds of drums.*

Much of the late 1950s and 1960s he spent at New York City's legendary Metropole Café; Gene played 18 weeks a year there until 1967. He's pictured here in front of their famed red curtain. Gene may have been trying a sizzle cymbal briefly during this engagement. It never reappeared.

From the Norman Granz and Downbeat *magazine archives comes a mid–1950s shot of Gene and Buddy. Rumors continue to abound that Norman Granz had film footage shot of Krupa and Rich doing their famed drum battle, as well as other "Jazz at the Philharmonic" players in action. Though film may exist, it hasn't yet turned up.*

Photograph from the collection of Duncan Schiedt.

The Great New Quartet *was the title of the Verve LP that featured this group—Charlie Ventura, "Knobby" Totah on bass and John Bunch on piano—shown here at the Embers in Indianapolis on March 28, 1964.*

Same group, unknown locale. Charlie Ventura, a star attraction on his own, really upped the entertainment value of the quartet.

LEADER
1. Henry Mancini ... 6,486
2. Stan Kenton ... 4,842
3. Duke Ellington ... 3,100
4. Count Basie ... 2,903
5. Maynard Ferguson ... 1,279
6. Quincy Jones ... 1,114
7. Woody Herman ... 917
8. Gerry Mulligan ... 912
9. Gil Evans ... 901
10. Dizzy Gillespie ... 725
11. Benny Goodman ... 698
12. Si Zentner ... 686
13. Nelson Riddle ... 491
14. Lionel Hampton ... 428
15. Gerald Wilson ... 410
16. Ray Conniff ... 377
17. Les Elgart ... 292
18. Les Brown ... 220
19. Billy May ... 212
20. Ted Heath ... 211
21. Pete Rugolo ... 177
22. Oliver Nelson ... 158
23. Harry James ... 149
24. Marty Paich ... 125
25. Ray McKinley ... 110
26. Shorty Rogers ... 104

TRUMPET
1. Miles Davis ... 17,283
2. Al Hirt ... 13,140
3. Dizzy Gillespie ... 11,390
4. Louis Armstrong ... 10,492
5. Maynard Ferguson ... 8,488
6. Jonah Jones ... 5,953
7. Nat Adderley ... 4,944
8. Bobby Hackett ... 4,262
9. Art Farmer ... 3,261
10. Billy Butterfield ... 2,926
11. Harry James ... 2,506
12. Shorty Rogers ... 2,390
13. Clark Terry ... 2,255
14. Doc Severinsen ... 1,555
15. Pete Candoli ... 1,311
16. Conte Candoli ... 1,242
17. Red Nichols ... 1,173
18. Roy Eldridge ... 1,149
19. Donald Byrd ... 1,043
20. Freddie Hubbard ... 825
21. Lee Morgan ... 807
22. Blue Mitchell ... 709
23. Don Cherry ... 690
24. Charlie Shavers ... 614
25. Wild Bill Davison ... 610
26. Jack Sheldon ... 568
27. Joe Newman ... 555
28. Buck Clayton ... 545
29. Kenny Dorham ... 497
30. Carmell Jones ... 483
31. Muggsy Spanier ... 452
32. Thad Jones ... 420
33. Ray Nance ... 401

TROMBONE
1. J. J. Johnson ... 17,780
2. Kai Winding ... 13,271
3. Si Zentner ... 9,605
4. Bob Brookmeyer ... 9,038
5. Jack Teagarden ... 8,522
6. Slide Hampton ... 4,588
7. Frank Rosolino ... 2,937
8. Urbie Green ... 2,824
9. Curtis Fuller ... 2,726
10. Turk Murphy ... 2,253
11. Jimmy Cleveland ... 2,043
12. J. C. Higginbotham ... 1,912
13. Kid Ory ... 1,825
14. Bennie Green ... 1,737
15. Dave Baker ... 1,733
16. Bill Harris ... 1,507
17. Milt Bernhart ... 1,462
18. Trummy Young ... 1,420
19. Carl Fontana ... 1,334
20. Tyree Glenn ... 1,285
21. Bob Fitzpatrick ... 1,284
22. Al Grey ... 1,249
23. Fred Assunto ... 1,095
24. Dick Nash ... 1,061
25. Quentin Jackson ... 968
26. Wilbur De Paris ... 906
27. Lawrence Brown ... 829
28. Wayne Henderson ... 777
29. Harry Betts ... 737
30. Benny Powell ... 728
31. Jimmy Knepper ... 652
32. Vic Dickenson ... 591
33. Melba Liston ... 492
34. Dickie Wells ... 487
35. Cutty Cutshall ... 479
36. Lou McGarity ... 477
37. Georg Brunis ... 435
37. Tommy Pederson ... 435

ALTO SAX
1. Cannonball Adderley 15,690
2. Paul Desmond ... 14,300
3. Earl Bostic ... 3,523
4. Johnny Hodges ... 2,305
5. Zoot Sims ... 1,758
6. Bud Shank ... 1,518
7. Ornette Coleman ... 1,362
8. Sonny Stitt ... 1,284
9. Paul Horn ... 1,155
10. Ted Nash ... 987
11. Lee Konitz ... 857
12. Benny Carter ... 792
13. Phil Woods ... 646
14. Jackie McLean ... 614
15. Hank Crawford ... 493
16. Eric Dolphy ... 491
17. James Moody ... 471
18. Charlie Mariano ... 440
19. Lennie Niehaus ... 406
20. Lou Donaldson ... 405
21. Al Belletto ... 338
22. Willie Smith ... 322
23. Herb Geller ... 308
24. Gabe Baltazar ... 282
25. Leo Wright ... 251
26. Jimmy Woods ... 236
27. Gigi Gryce ... 223
28. Walt Levinsky ... 222
29. John Handy ... 216

TENOR SAX
1. Stan Getz ... 16,287
2. John Coltrane ... 8,178
3. Sonny Rollins ... 4,259
4. Coleman Hawkins ... 3,740
5. Zoot Sims ... 1,836
6. "Fathead" Newman ... 1,588
7. Al Cohn ... 1,095
8. Yusef Lateef ... 1,023
9. Bud Freeman ... 956
10. Eddie Davis ... 852
11. Eddie Harris ... 849
12. Roland Kirk ... 848
13. Ben Webster ... 842
14. Paul Gonsalves ... 782
15. Georgie Auld ... 760
16. Dave Pell ... 733
17. Sonny Stitt ... 687
18. Sam Donahue ... 675
19. Illinois Jacquet ... 674
20. Buddy Tate ... 610
21. Vido Musso ... 603
22. Jimmy Heath ... 597
23. Hank Mobley ... 530
24. James Moody ... 486
25. Bob Cooper ... 481
26. Bill Perkins ... 392
27. Flip Phillips ... 388
28. Eddie Miller ... 385
29. Richie Kamuca ... 360
30. Stanley Turrentine ... 345
31. Plas Johnson ... 339
32. Sal Nistico ... 323
33. Al Klink ... 307
34. Bill Holman ... 253
35. Budd Johnson ... 251
36. Benny Golson ... 223
37. Teddy Edwards ... 212

BARITONE SAX
1. Gerry Mulligan ... 19,667
2. Jimmy Giuffre ... 1,585
3. Bud Shank ... 1,093
4. Pepper Adams ... 1,040
5. Charles Davis ... 778
6. Harry Carney ... 762
7. Chuck Gentry ... 628
8. Sahib Shihab ... 526
9. Cecil Payne ... 506
10. Frank Hittner ... 474
11. Lonnie Shaw ... 414
12. Jerome Richardson ... 391
13. Bill Hood ... 341
14. Ernie Caceres ... 273
15. Stanley Webb ... 237

CLARINET
1. Pete Fountain ... 9,447
2. Benny Goodman ... 4,111
3. Acker Bilk ... 2,816
4. Buddy DeFranco ... 2,786
5. Jimmy Giuffre ... 2,675
6. Woody Herman ... 2,436
7. Paul Horn ... 1,030
8. Pee Wee Russell ... 781
9. Buddy Collette ... 747
10. Jimmy Hamilton ... 409
11. Tony Scott ... 408
12. Phil Woods ... 261
13. Bill Smith ... 239
14. Edmond Hall ... 233
15. Sol Yaged ... 217
16. Barney Bigard ... 214
17. Matty Matlock ... 213
18. Peanuts Hucko ... 137
19. Phil Bodner ... 122

PIANO
1. Dave Brubeck ... 6,747
2. Oscar Peterson ... 2,941
3. André Previn ... 2,785
4. Peter Nero ... 2,586
5. Erroll Garner ... 1,916
6. Ahmad Jamal ... 1,604
7. George Shearing ... 1,436
8. Thelonious Monk ... 1,423
9. Bill Evans ... 822
10. Count Basie ... 779
11. Duke Ellington ... 755
12. Ramsey Lewis ... 622
13. Les McCann ... 458
14. John Lewis ... 452
15. Horace Silver ... 386
16. Don Shirley ... 353
17. Vince Guaraldi ... 331
18. Wynton Kelly ... 294
19. Teddy Wilson ... 245
20. Mose Allison ... 222
21. Eddie Heywood ... 210
22. Pete Jolly ... 203
23. Bobby Timmons ... 143
24. Earl "Fatha" Hines ... 130
25. Phineas Newborn, Jr. ... 127
26. Steve Allen ... 115
27. Bud Powell ... 112
28. McCoy Tyner ... 111
29. Billy Taylor ... 109
30. Red Garland ... 107

GUITAR
1. Charlie Byrd ... 6,800
2. Chet Atkins ... 6,788
3. Wes Montgomery ... 2,181
4. Barney Kessel ... 1,985
5. Laurindo Almeida ... 1,612
6. Kenny Burrell ... 1,301
7. Jim Hall ... 1,066
8. Herb Ellis ... 1,044
9. Eddie Condon ... 937
10. Les Paul ... 870
11. Johnny Smith ... 813
12. Tony Mottola ... 600
13. Al Viola ... 491
14. Mundell Lowe ... 412
15. Sal Salvador ... 382
16. Al Hendrickson ... 333
17. Joe Pass ... 279
18. Freddie Green ... 255
19. George Van Eps ... 245
20. Grant Green ... 206
21. Tal Farlow ... 177
22. Oscar Moore ... 167
23. Howard Roberts ... 125
24. Bill Harris ... 122
25. Barry Galbraith ... 100

BASS
1. Ray Brown ... 6,487
2. Charlie Mingus ... 4,460
3. Gene Wright ... 2,500
4. Paul Chambers ... 1,443
5. Art Davis ... 966
6. Buddy Clark ... 904
7. Percy Heath ... 869
8. Chubby Jackson ... 737
9. Leroy Vinnegar ... 722
10. Norman Bates ... 696
11. Bob Haggart ... 681
12. Red Mitchell ... 677
13. Sam Jones ... 628
14. Don Bagley ... 591
15. Eddie Safranski ... 575
16. Milt Hinton ... 491
17. El Dee Young ... 424
18. Keter Betts ... 417
19. Arvell Shaw ... 400
20. Monk Montgomery ... 336
21. Slam Stewart ... 327
22. Pops Foster ... 266
23. George Duvivier ... 245
24. Howard Rumsey ... 231
25. Bill Crow ... 225
25. Gary Peacock ... 225
27. Ron Carter ... 186
28. Johnny Frigo ... 182
29. Eddie Jones ... 180
30. Mike Rubin ... 174
31. Joe Benjamin ... 153
32. Monty Budwig ... 148
33. Joe Mondragon ... 145
34. Red Callender ... 135
35. George Tucker ... 113

DRUMS
1. Joe Morello ... 7,241
2. Shelly Manne ... 3,900
3. Gene Krupa ... 3,784
4. Art Blakey ... 2,134
5. Cozy Cole ... 1,849
6. Buddy Rich ... 1,200
7. Max Roach ... 1,069
8. Philly Joe Jones ... 1,015
9. Chico Hamilton ... 909
10. Ed Thigpen ... 543
11. Louis Bellson ... 516
12. Jo Jones ... 483
13. Rufus Jones ... 422
14. Elvin Jones ... 397

180

By 1964, according to the Playboy *magazine jazz poll, the name of Gene Krupa was still way up there among the public. Only Joe Morello and Shelly Manne came in ahead of him. Buddy Rich placed sixth. Buddy could not have been happy.*

The quartet on a 1965 Dean Martin Show *with Bennie Moten on bass, Carmen Leggio on tenor saxophone and (probably) Dick Wellstood on piano.*

About 1969, during his retirement, coaching the local baseball team named for him. That's long time colleague Frank Belinno next to Gene. Gene was very much involved in charity work on behalf of the mentally disabled though the years, and Frank Bellinno announced the establishment of the Gene Krupa Memorial Fund for Retarded Children, after Gene's death in 1973.

THE 1970s

Fans of that "ace drummer man," and there were many, were thrilled at the news that he had decided to come out of retirement. One of his first dates was at a club located within New York City's Plaza Hotel, called Plaza Nine and All That Jazz. During that engagement, the Gene Krupa Quartet consisted of Eddie Shu on saxophones, harmonica and trumpet; Dick Wellstood on piano, and Scotty Holt on bass. Gene was back, slower and pacing himself carefully, but so much more musical.

Jim Chapin and Joe Morello, among others, visited Krupa at his Yonkers home during the retirement years and gave him lessons. He continued to evolve and continued to move along musically. As usual, he gave his sidemen plenty of room to stretch out (Eddie Shu was demonstrating a decidedly "Coltrane influence" at that time) and never told them how or what to play. The Krupa groups were a blending together of various jazz styles, although no matter what they played or how they played it, the quartet was always identifiable as a Gene Krupa-led outfit.

There was a return to his roots at this time as well. Around 1970, Gene began appearing as "special guest star" with mainstream/Dixieland outfits of a regional orientation, such as Chuck Slate's Jazz Band from New Jersey, and The Six-Star International Jazz Band, led by Al Winters, out of Detroit. In the New England area, Gilbert Yule booked Gene for benefits at various private schools in New England, including the Forman and Hotchkiss Schools in Connecticut. Gil Yule, a devoted friend, fan, and colleague of Gene's, has a 1971 itinerary of Gene's that would rival his activity in the 1950s. In addition, he made regular concert and festival appearances with the again-assembled Benny Goodman Quartet; got together with the Eddie Condon "Chicago Gang" for several concerts including one memorable one that was recorded at New York's New School; played Radio City Music Hall as a part of the Newport Jazz Festival; filmed a couple of television specials in Canada (one had another Krupa/Rich drum battle); and appeared in and around the New York City area with his own group and a Dixie-type outfit called Balaban and Cats. The vast majority of these concerts and club dates have been undocumented in any Krupa discography—offical or unofficial—until recently. And, he continued his appearances on behalf of the Slingerland Drum Company as well as lecturing in schools on, as he described it, "the narcotics thing."

Then there were the ceremonial occasions: A party that Buddy Rich gave for Gene in New York City was attended by everyone from Jerry Lewis to Zutty Singleton. He was the first drummer ever elected to the induction as the *Down Beat* magazine "Hall of Fame." And during a concert at the Singer Bowl outside of New York City, Jo Jones presented a plaque to Gene that was signed, with gratitude, by every living "name" jazz drummer.

His final days couldn't have been easy. His beloved Yonkers home was badly damaged by fire in early 1973, he had back problems, hearing problems, heart problems, emphysema, and something called "benign leukemia" that was treated successfully for a time via regular blood transfusions. His wife, Pat, left him and took the children. "What else. . . what else can happened to me?" Gene asked of his friend, pianist Marty Napoleon.

With all that, he continued to play, and play very, very well, up until less than two months before he died. The Original Benny Goodman Quartet with all the original members performed for the final time on August 18, 1973 at Saratoga. Gene died on October 16 at the age of 64.

Gene reunited with Charlie Ventura at a Philadelphia night spot called Brandi's Wharf in 1970. Eddie Shu was there, too, but since Ventura was living and playing in Philadelphia, he invited Charlie to join the band for the weekend engagement. Pianist is Jay Jason from New York and the unknown bassist was from Philadelphia. Note the "updated" Slingerlands with the double bass drum spurs. He still opted for old-style "flat base" cymbal stands and tilters. Yes, that's Gene Krupa's signature.

Elder statesman of the drums, filmed at a midnight jam session at Radio City Music Hall as a part of the 1972 Newport Jazz Festival.

143

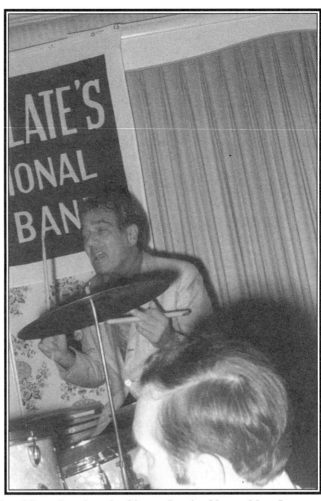

Gene in action during a 1970s date with Chuck Slate's Traditional Jazz Band at the Chester Inn in Chester New Jersey.

Chuck Slate, Jr., who provided these photos, was there: "My father called Eddie Condon to get Gene's phone number for the 1970 weekend gig. He was nervous, as Gene was his idol for so long, and suddenly here is his home phone number. Well, he called and Gene was there, and what followed was a great conversation. Gene said he would do the two-day gig. He said that Gene was so nice, just like everyone who really knew him had always said. He said he hadn't been well, so when my father asked if he could bring his drum set and maybe they could do something together at some point, Gene said he wasn't up to that, but would sit in during the course of each evening and play with my father's band. He stayed at our house for the weekend, and I remember meeting him. I was eight years old at the time and had to give my room up to him. He was drumming on our kitchen table and just hung out during the day in the house before the two appearances. Shortly after his death in 1973, I turned on the television, and there was a show he had done in the last couple years of his life. He dashed on stage, and I recall getting tears in my eyes, having thought back to the time at our house and what a nice guy he was, and the fact that he was gone. He was a special person."

144

The Goodman Quartet (left to right) Goodman, Teddy Wilson, Lionel Hampton, Gene, filmed for a PBS television special in 1972 at Lincoln Center. Goodman was the only one to insist that they be recorded "live." Count Basie and Duke Ellington, also at the concert, mimed for the TV special.

At one of the Canadian television specials, around 1971.

"World of Music" tribute to Lionel Hampton at New York City's Waldorf–Astoria in 1973.

Playing "Them There Eyes" with a group of Connecticut jazzers at The Hotchkiss School on May 7, 1972.

Getting ready for his solo on "Lester Leaps In" at The Forman School in Connecticut, on May 29, 1971. This wonderful concert was recorded and pressed on to about 50 "limited edition private" LPs. It is now available from JazzLegends.com.

At the Chimney Sweep Restaurant in Canton, Connecticut; on January 10, 1972. Gene was quite busy in the New England area at this time, often appearing with the Balaban & Cats dixie-oriented ensemble. That's presumably Balaban at the bass. Gene made no secret of the fact that he had a number of health problems at this time. His friend, drummer Johnny Vine (those are Vine's drums), often played on several numbers per set to ensure that Gene didn't over extend himself.

Buddy Rich threw a big party for Gene at a New York City restaurant on August 15, 1973. Buddy wanted to show his love and appreciation for Gene "while he was still around." Here's Jerry Lewis, Gene and Buddy.

The two most famous drummers who ever lived: (right to left) Krupa and Rich.

Jo Jones, at the same party, giving his long-time friend an award.

Anyone who knew Buddy Rich was aware that he was a sentimental softie at heart, here with a tear in his eye. He loved Gene, and they actually had plans to take a vacation together shortly after this party. It never happened. Gene's last appearance was three days after this party at Saratoga with the Goodman Quartet, and he was just too ill to travel by then.

ENDORSEMENTS

William F. Ludwig, Jr. told drum historian/author Rob Cook that Gene's connection with Slingerland began after the Goodman band's hit engagement at the Congress Hotel in Chicago. Krupa supposedly had been playing Ludwig drums purchased by his father at Chicago's biggest music store, Lyon and Healy. Dad wanted his son to have new drums after the success at the Congress, so he called the Ludwig company on the phone and unfortunately got the brush off. Going to the yellow pages, Mr. Krupa found a listing for the Slingerland Banjo and Drum Company and talked to H.H. Slingerland, and Gene got a white marine pearl outfit for a wholesale price. Gene Krupa played and endorsed Slingerland drums continuously for 38 years and was featured on the cover of every Slingerland drum catalog from 1936 until 1967.

He was responsible for a number of manufacturing innovations at Slingerland, including tunable tom toms, the development of the ever-popular Radio King snare drum, and the concept of "streamlining" the drum kit. He used four or five drums, four cymbals and a hi-hat. It was a set of drums shorn of temple blocks, effects, whistles, bells and gadgets that were a part of the drummer's arsenal for so many years. In effect, Gene Krupa helped invent what we now know as the drumset.

He must have helped sell thousands of Slingerlands over the years, and beginning in 1947, signed a 10-year deal with them that gave him a share of the profits from every drum sold. He deserved it.

Sizes may have changed through the years, bass drums, specifically, became smaller, but they were *always* Slingerland.

In those days, drummers used either cheap brass cymbals from China or Zildjians. Gene was with Zildjan from the start. Jon Cohan, in his wonderful book *Zildjian: A History of the Legendary Cymbal Makers*, says that Avedis Zildjian first met Gene by way of a New York drum shop owner named Bill Mather. Armand Zildjian told Cohan that the first Istanbul Ks, in Krupa's estimation, were too heavy. Armand said, "Gene loved [my] old man, they were real good buddies. And [Gene] said, 'Can you make the cymbals thinner?' Nobody made thin cymbals, so we made what was called the Paper Thin. Gene suggested a thinner cymbal. That's very important because that's what got the whole thing going right."

Again, the sizes changed over the years—cymbals got larger while drums got smaller—but without exception, they were Zildjians.

One of the earliest trade ads for Gene and Slingerland. For 10 cents—postpaid—Slingerland would send you an 8 by 10 "action photograph" of Gene Krupa.

The Latest Trend
is Soft Rhythms
with

GENE KRUPA

and his

**SLINGERLAND
"RADIO KINGS"**

Send for assortment of
8 x 10 glossy photographs
of leading drummers in
action for 10c each post-
paid.

The news has it that Gene's music has undergone a
great change. Asked why he's switched from ear-splitting
to soft-rhythms, he explains: "If we play loud all night
no one will know the difference when we blow our ears
out. But when we use dynamics and build up our fortissimo
. . . they really know it." His band is a science with Gene—
that's why there can be no substitute for Slingerland Radio
Kings. Do as the nation's Foremost Drummer does — be
sure it's a Slingerland. Remember his choice is Slingerland.

NGERLAND DRUM CO.

A year or so later, espousing that the latest trend is soft rhythms. As the copy states, "If we play loud all night no one will know the difference when we blow our ears out. But if you use dynamics and build up our fortissimo. . . they really know it."

In an ad for Robins Music Corporation, offering four of the band's early charts for sale at 75 cents each. Robbins also published Gene's first instructional book, The Gene Krupa Drum Method, then selling for two dollars.

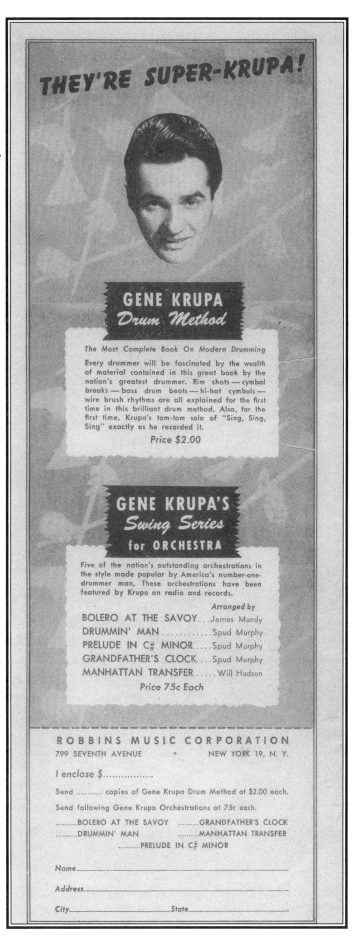

Every band had to play its share of novelties, vocal charts and pop tunes of the day. The Krupa band was no exception as the cover to the sheet music of Harriet, *"a western novelty song," demonstrates.*

For Slingerland and War Bonds, hyping the "Rolling Bomber" line of drums, "Built along the same, identical lines (as Radio Kings), with only a few modifications in design because of war time restrictions. Only a small percentage of metal could be used in the manufacture of drums during the war years. Even the lugs were made of wood.

"I have have used Slingerland Radio Kings for over 10 years," the ad says. "Having tried other makes, I know Slingerland is the only make for me." This comes from the early 1950s.

A different version of the above, this was Slingerland's ad that appeared in the Jazz at the Philharmonic program, proclaiming Gene as the "world's greatest drummer."

Late 1950s Slingerland ad featuring some new and innovative products. Gene is described here as "the world's most famous drummer."

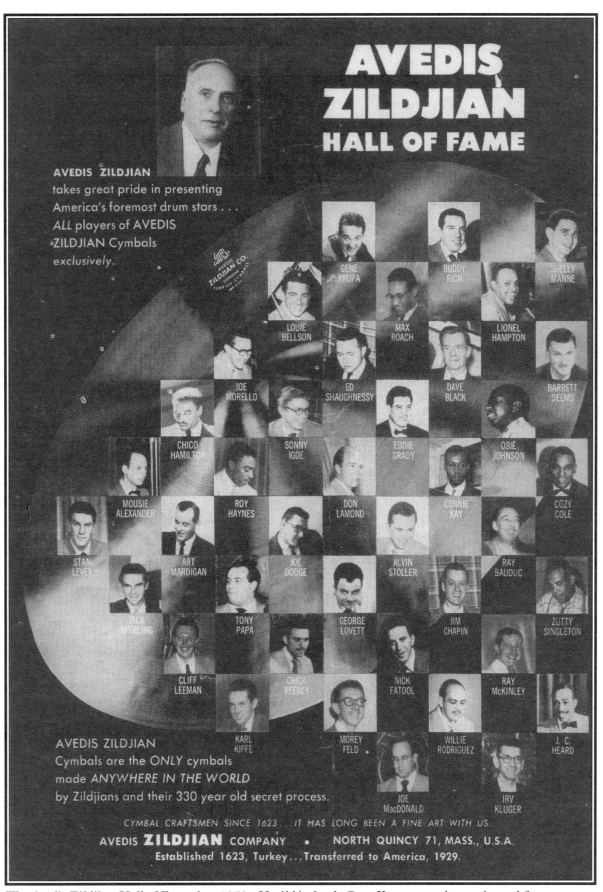

The Avedis Zildjian Hall of Fame, late 1950s. Until his death, Gene Krupa was always pictured first.

Those are actually Buddy Rich's drums, and the photo was taken at the Avedis Zildjian factory around 1972 for Gene's final Zildjian photo shoot. In the last book of Zildjian Cymbal Set-ups that featured Gene, his cymbals were said to consist of 14-inch new beat hi-hats, an 18-inch crash to the left, a 20-inch ride mounted on the bass drum; another 18-inch crash to his right, and a 22-inch swish to the right of that. It looked great on paper, but at that time, Gene never had two cymbals to his right (it was usually just the swish), and someone left out the splash cymbal mounted on the bass drum that he had as a part of his cymbal set up for almost 40 years.

Gene with Avedis Zildjian, 1972.

Bob Grauso, founder of the original Fibes Drum Company, built this snare drum especially for Gene Krupa in the late 1960s. The original Fibes drums, made of fiberglass as their name indicates, were wonderful instruments, and Grauso reportedly made a number of these custom jobs for other "name" drummers. Grauso used Fibes shells, but covered them in the drummers' favorite finish with hardware from whatever actual brand of drum the player was endorsing. Hence, this is a Fibes shell with Slingerland covering and Slingerland hardware, a duplication of a Gene Krupa drum right down to the holes left by the removal of the internal muffler. This classic was presented by Gene Krupa to Chuck Slate in July, 1970.

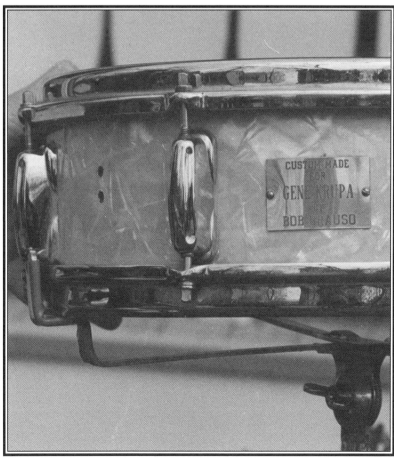

**"America's Ace Drummer Man"...
The Pioneer of the Modern Drum Set....**

Gene Krupa
A Slingerland Legend

Gene Krupa started it all. Working with Slingerland engineers, he inspired the invention of the tunable tom tom and made the Radio King Snare famous. His musical genius inspired thousands of drummers to follow in his footsteps. Most important of all, Gene elevated the very role of the modern drummer – from a seldom-noticed timekeeper to a creative artist and musical celebrity.

Gene Krupa knew quality when he saw it. And he played Slingerland drums <u>exclusively</u> until the end of his life. Now, you too can own a piece of drumming history. To kick off our 70th year, Slingerland announces the Gene Krupa™ Signature Drum Kit – part of the new Slingerland Legends Series.

Official Drum set of the New Gene Krupa Big Band (shown here with optional 16x18 floor tom). Configuration is based on Gene Krupa's preferences; variations are available by special order.

70th ANNIVERSARY
Slingerland
Legends Series

The legacy lives through the "new" Slingerland Drum Company and their Krupa tribute outfit. As the ad correctly reads, "Gene Krupa started it all."

Finale of the 1938 Carnegie Hall Jazz concert, immortalized in French "comic book" form by artist Oliver Desvaux.
Frame used by permission of Bruno Theol and Editions Nocturne.

Desvaux's rendering of Gene and the new band he put together in 1944 after leaving Tommy Dorsey. Frame used by permission of Bruno Theol and Editions Nocturne.

WORLD OF *Gene Krupa*

BRUCE H. KLAUBER

THAT LEGENDARY DRUMMIN' MAN

WITH AN INTRODUCTION BY MEL TORMÉ

Cover to 1990's World of Gene Krupa, *the first serious book on Gene.*

Gene's famed appearance on the second season of The Dean Martin Show, *aired September 22, 1966.*

GENE AND I

My interest in Gene Krupa, drums and jazz began when I was eight years old. I heard records by the 1937–1938 Benny Goodman band and was absolutely mesmerized by the force, drive, swing and enthusiasm of that legendary ensemble, specifically by the excitement generated by the drummer. Inspired by what I heard, I began taking drum lessons. This was in 1961, when jazz was going through a popularity surge. The Brubeck Quartet was riding high on college campuses, jazz was played regularly on the radio, Maynard Ferguson was the hippest band around, there were actually such things as "jazz clubs" bringing in star names frequently, and I'm told that even neighborhood restaurants and bars were booking jazz trios. There was plenty of jazz around. As an example, a 1960 concert at Philadelphia's Academy of Music had a show comprised of the Horace Silver Quintet, the Johnny Griffin/Lockjaw Davis group with Shirley Scott on organ, and the big bands of Maynard Ferguson and Count Basie, with noted jazz radio personality Sid Mark as the master of ceremonies. Jazz was "in," jazz was "hip," jazz was being played on the new stereo systems of suburbanites, and to the public at large, along with Joe Morello (remember that *Take Five* was actually a "hit" record) Gene Krupa and Buddy Rich were still "the world's greatest drummers."

As I became more involved in the study of drums I quickly learned that Gene hadn't been at the cutting edge of jazz for some time, and like many percussion students, I was blown away when I first heard Buddy Rich. But a certain "something" kept drawing me to Gene. I saw him on television on many occasions, and in person for the first time at a taping of the Philadelphia-based *Mike Douglas Show* and subsequently at the Steel Pier, the Plaza Hotel, Brandi's Wharf in Philadelphia and at the 1972 Newport Jazz Festival.

I wondered why he was on the *Tonight Show* and not Art Blakey, Morello or Max Roach. How was Gene Krupa able to appeal to hard core jazz fans *and* a wider public who didn't like jazz before or since Gene? And what was it about this guy that would inspire Columbia Pictures to make a story about his life? How did this drummer—this jazz drummer—become a star? Maybe, just maybe, if I kept up with my music studies and could figure out just what this guy had, then I could be a big-time jazz drumming celebrity, too.

Some have said that Gene's style was simple and understandable, not over the heads of Mr. and Mrs. Public. Others maintain that his showmanship, his ability to project and to draw people in, were the keys to his popularity. I've learned this: Charisma can't be analyzed or duplicated or imitated. And charisma is what Gene had. Sinatra had it, and Buddy Rich had it. Not too many others in or out of music have. This was a special power, and Gene was among the few to use this power wisely. "In his commitment to real jazz," musicologist Gunther Schuller wrote in his book, *The Swing Era*, "even in its more advanced bop manifestation, Krupa, with his fame, brought first-rate modern jazz to untold numbers of listeners who would otherwise never have had contact with it…Given the vagaries of the commercial world in which jazz has always had to fight for its survival, clearly this was no small achievement."

Were there "better" drummers in jazz history? Faster? More modern? Flashier? More innovative and versatile? Maybe. But they were not Gene Krupa.

ABOUT THE AUTHOR

Photo courtesy of Joe Adams

Bruce H. Klauber is a writer, author, editor, producer, jazz educator, recording artist, drummer and multi-instrumentalist. He has contributed to dozens of national music periodicals, is the author of *World of Gene Krupa: That Legendary Drummin' Man*, producer and writer of the DCI Music Videos on Krupa, Buddy Rich and The Legends of Jazz Drumming. He is currently Hudson Music's Jazz Legends Series Producer, teacher of Music Journalism at Philadelphia's University of the Arts, and Musical Director for noted jazz singer Joy Adams.

Gene and former boss—soon to again, briefly become his boss—Benny Goodman. This still is from jam session sequence from the 1942 film "Syncopation." Others in this famed clip were winners of the Saturday Evening Post's *reader poll for "All American Jazz Band." Bandleader/trombonist Tommy Dorsey.*

COMPANION CD

The eight tracks on this CD cover five decades of Krupa drumming in a variety of situations. Though some of this material has been floating around among collectors through the years, none of it has ever been issued commercially in CD form. The majority of these certifiable collectors items have Gene and the groups playing live. Like most jazz musicians of any era, Gene Krupa really gave his all before a live audience.

"Wire Brush Stomp" comes to us courtesy of Krupa collector Robert Bierman. This was recorded as a radio promotional piece for the 1938 film that starred Gene and Bob Hope, called "Some Like it Hot," later retitled "Rhythm Romance." Krupa was a natural for motion pictures, and this was the first one in which he appeared without Benny Goodman and his Orchestra. This interesting track is the actual drum part to "Stomp" as played in the film, without the orchestra. Listen to his wonderful sense of time.

"Stompin' at the Savoy" was a staple of all the Krupa groups through the years. This version, by the Krupa Jazz Trio and introduced by Groucho Marx, clocks in at 4:45. By the 1960s, some live renditions of it lasted nearly 20 minutes.

"The Galloping Comedians" appeared on the 1961 "Classics in Percussion," a.k.a. "Percussion King" session for Verve. This was actually one of several "semi-classical" pieces Gene commissioned for his 1949 band from arranger George "The Fox" Williams and was among the Krupa band's final dates for Columbia. Gene had a life-long interest in classical music and regretted that he never formally appeared in a symphonic setting.

"Idaho" and "Dark Eyes" are two exciting tracks recorded live at the Band Box in New York City in 1953. After he broke up his big band, Gene went back to the trio format with Charlie Ventura and Teddy Napoleon that had been featured as an "added attraction" within the big band. Ventura had become quite the "name" since leaving Gene around 1946, particularly with his famed, "Bop for the People" combo. While this is unquestionably a "swing trio," you can hear the many bop touches from the tenor sax of Charlie.

Television host Steve Allen was pegged to play the lead in the 1955 film, *The Benny Goodman Story*, and many of his TV shows that year were devoted to the musicians who appeared in the film. This is one of those programs, and Gene really tears it up here on "Indiana" and a blues.

"Sing, Sing, Sing" is a television performance from 1960, featuring one of Krupa's most musical groups. Eddie Wasserman, with the drummer for six years, was a Julliard graduate, fluent on tenor saxophone, clarinet and flute. He was also one of the biggest musical contractors in New York City, and was responsible for assembling the players for the famed, Krupa versus Rich record date entitled "Burnin' Beat." English pianist Ronnie Ball studied with Lennie Tristano and was active with a number of modernists. Bassist is likely Jimmy Gannon, a busy New York player who worked with Woody Herman. Gannon was also the first bassist recruited by Buddy

Rich when Buddy put together his big band in 1966. Gene and Buddy shared a lot of players through the years.

"Caravan" and "Big Noise From Winnetka" were recordings made solely as promotional sessions for The National Guard. Also on these transcriptions was Tony Bennett, along with veteran "Make Believe Ballroom" host Martin Block (Block breaks in with an ID on "Big Noise"). Gene loved to play "Caravan," and in person, would really stretch out on it. In fact, he commissioned Quincy Jones to write a big band chart on it, based on this arrangement. It was never recorded commercially, though it was performed by Gene during a 1962 *Tonight Show* guest spot. "Big Noise," a hit for drummer Ray Bauduc and bassist Bob Haggart, was a real crowd-pleaser, especially during the section when he played drumsticks on the bass players' bass strings.

"Leave Us Leap" is the 1971 version of what was one of the Krupa band's biggest hits when first recorded in 1945. Gene was more active in the 1970-1973 period than any discography or chronology indicated. This Canadian television appearance with Guido Basso and the orchestra around 1971 is just one example of how busy he was, and how great he sounded up until the end.

For more information on these and other rare Krupa titles, visit us on the web at JazzLegends.com (http://www.jazzlegends.com).